MOOCs and Open Education
A Special Issue of the International Journal on E-Learning

Edited by

MIMI MIYOUNG LEE
University of Houston, USA
mlee7@uh.edu

CURTIS J. BONK
Indiana University, USA
cjbonk@indiana.edu

THOMAS H. REYNOLDS
National University, USA
treynold@nu.edu

THOMAS C. REEVES
The University of Georgia, USA
treeves@uga.edu

INTERNATIONAL JOURNAL ON E-LEARNING
Special Issue: MOOCs and Open Education

Volume 14, Number 3	2015

Articles

*The International Journal on E-Learning (ISSN# 1537-2456) is published by the Association for
the Advancement of Computing in Education (AACE), an international, educational, nonprofit
organization. Subscription Rates: (U.S. Funds on U.S. Bank, international money order, AMEX,
MC, VISA, or Discover.) Annual subscription rate is $125. Annual Library subscription rate is
$195 (U.S.). Add $15 for non-U.S. postage. To subscribe online: www.aace.org/subs*

*Publisher: AACE, PO Box 719, Waynesville, NC, 28786, USA
E-mail: info@aace.org © Copyright 2015 by AACE.
Published Quarterly • website: http://www.aace.org*

*Indexed in: Educational Research Abstracts, ERIC,
EdITLib-Education and Information Technology Digital Library, Index Copernicus,
GetCited, Google Scholar, Journal Seek, Microsoft Academic Search,
Bacon's Media Directory, Cabell's, Ulrich, and several others*

International Jl. on E-Learning (2015) **14**(3) Special Issue, 265-277

Preface to MOOCs and Open Education Special Issue: The Power of Four

CURTIS J. BONK
Indiana University, USA
cjbonk@indiana.edu

MIMI MIYOUNG LEE
University of Houston, USA
mlee7@uh.edu

THOMAS H. REYNOLDS
National University, USA
treynold@nu.edu

THOMAS C. REEVES
The University of Georgia, USA
treeves@uga.edu

In April of 2001, the president of MIT, Charles Vest, announced the establishment of a project for placing MIT course contents on the Web for free. In effect, this announcement started the OpenCourseWare (OCW) movement. Since that time, massive open online courses (MOOCs) and open educational resources (OER) have proliferated on the scene. A flurry of research reports, books, programs, announcements, debates, and conferences related to MOOCs and open education have forced educators to reflect on how these new forms of educational delivery might enhance or even transform education. In response, the four editors of this special issue, Mimi Lee, Curt Bonk, Tom Reynolds, and Tom Reeves, organized a preconference symposium on this topic at the International E-Learn Conference in Las Vegas in October 2013 which resulted in this special issue. This particular article serves as the preface to the special issue.

INTRODUCTION

On April 4, 2001, Charles Vest, then president of MIT, announced the establishment of an OpenCourseWare (OCW) project on his campus (MIT News, 2001). Part of what Vest said was:

> "As president of MIT, I have come to expect top-level innovative and intellectually entrepreneurial ideas from the MIT community. When we established the Council on Educational Technology at MIT, we charged a sub-group with coming up with a project that reached beyond our campus classrooms.
>
> I have to tell you that we went into this expecting that something creative, cutting-edge and challenging would emerge. And, frankly, we also expected that it would be something based on a revenue-producing model -- a project or program that took into account the power of the Internet and its potential for new applications in education...OpenCourseWare combines two things: the traditional openness and outreach and democratizing influence of American education and the ability of the Web to make vast amounts of information instantly available."

There are several interesting comments in the above excerpt of his statement. For one, Vest rightfully indicates that the field of educational technology is having a significant impact in university strategic planning. Second, for the most part, in terms of online forms of education, the free and open world won out over the for-profit one. And, third, there are vast amounts of courses and other information resources freely available today from universities and other educational entities that previously were unheard of or deemed impossible. Perhaps even more remarkable, within seven years of Vest's bold proclamation, content from more than 90 percent of MIT 2,000+ courses was available for anyone in the world to explore and study at any time and from any place with an Internet connection (MIT Press Release, 2007). And explore they did.

Extensive planning, piloting, and financial resources combined with flexible instructional design approaches, highly prominent marketing and communication, and faculty commitment resulted in millions of people browsing or downloading content from the MIT OCW site each month (S. E. Carson, personal communication, January 14, 2014). Clearly, OCW is fulfilling its intention to be a "broad-based movement that would impact knowledge, information and education worldwide" (MIT Press Release, 2007).

OCW was not limited to MIT, however. Instead, other leading universities in the United States such as Johns Hopkins, Yale, Tufts, and Notre Dame quickly joined in the open education movement with their own versions of OCW, as did dozens of other universities around the world (Carson, 2009; Caswell, Henson, Jensen, & Wiley, 2007).

Anyone exploring the Web today will quickly realize that OCW is only part of the open education movement; in fact, there are also learning portals, open access journal articles, open educational resource repositories, and other types of open educational resources (OER) from which to learn. For example, for those interested in Western thought and literature, the complete works of Ernest Hemmingway, Jane Austin, William Shakespeare, Albert Einstein, Mary Shelley, and Charles Darwin, among thousands of other key historical figures, can be accessed and searched online (Bonk, 2009). What is vital to point out is that these learning portals have the potential to shift the balance of power from teachers and content providers to those seeking to learn from them.

MOOCS AND OER: CRITICISMS, ISSUES, AND POSSIBILITIES

Arguably, we are on the cusp of a new age of learner-centered and learner-selected learning. Research is now needed on the motivations, challenges, and successes of those learning from OER, OCW, and other emerging forms of online learning delivery (Bonk, Lee, Kou, Xu, & Sheu, 2015). Realizing this potential will not be easy or automatic. For example, a recent survey (FTI Consulting, 2015) sponsored by the Gates Foundation showed that most faculty members were aware of technological innovations such as OER and OCW, but relatively few were using them in their teaching. Worse, in a study of higher education teaching faculty in the United States, Allen and Seaman (2014) found that most were unaware of what OER even was. And, of those who were aware, most of those surveyed indicated that time to find and evaluate this content was a major barrier to use of OER. At the same time, when presented with the concept of OER, most of these faculty members indicated that would be willing to incorporate OER into their instruction.

Contrast that with a recent international study from the OER Research Hub at the Open University (OU) Institute of Educational Technology (de los Arcos, Farrow, Perryman, Pitt, & Weller, 2014) of more than 1,000 educators and nearly 5,000 formal and informal learners. In this study, nearly 80 percent of these educators indicated that they used OER to acquire new ideas and inspiration. It is also important to point out that the more educators used OER, the more likely that they were willing to share resources with others. Notably, most formal learners in this study believed that they saved money from OER. In addition, roughly thirty percent of informal learners indicated that the use of OER influenced their decision to sign up for a course. The vast majority of OER users, whether formal or informal, adopted these resources to fit their personal needs. Another finding worth noting is that of the types of free and open materials available, videos were the most commonly used.

OER and OCW are just part of the equation. Today, the term MOOCs or "massive open online courses" is part of the everyday lexicon related to the use of educational technology in higher education. It is generally accepted that the MOOC trend started in 2008 in Canada and swiftly spread to the United States and many other parts of the world. In addition to MIT, universities such as Stanford University, Duke University, the University of Pennsylvania, the University of Michigan, the UK Open University, and the University of Edinburgh, were among the key early adapters, all of whom made concerted efforts to conduct research on their MOOCs (e.g., Belanger & Thornton, 2013; Christensen, Steinmetz, Alcorn, Bennett, & Woods, 2013; MOOC @ Edinburgh 2013 – Report #1, 2013). At the same time that universities were piloting this ground-breaking form of educational delivery and people within those universities were examining and debating the many MOOC announcements and reports that were appearing, MOOC-related courses and programs, software companies, and governmental initiatives arose to fill in the gap of services that were then needed. Entities such as Udacity, Udemy, edX, NovoEd, Open2Study, FutureLearn, and Coursera were often the focus of stories in both the academic and popular press, although these stories ranged from enthusiastic endorsements (Pappano, 2012) to withering criticisms (Drake, 2014).

Clearly, MOOCs mean different things to different people. For some, MOOCs allow unique opportunities to diversify one's student base. For others, the emphasis is on the creation of global learning communities that share ideas, resources, and best practices. Still others view MOOCs as a tool for expanding access to education. New acronyms are proliferating, including MOOCs related to connectivist theory (i.e., cMOOCs), MOOCs that seem to focus on the quantity of students or throughput (i.e., xMOOCS), ones that entail insightful experimentations with project- and problem-based learning (i.e., pMOOCs), and MOOCs for professional development such as teacher educators, business executives, or medical personnel (i.e., PD-MOOCs) (Bonk, Lee, Reeves, & Reynolds, 2015b; Laurillard, 2014). And as shown in the article by Shoba Bandi-Rao and Christopher Devers in this special issue, there are now opportunities for MOOCs to address remedial education such as basic reading and writing skills. Still other forms of MOOCs and open education relate to advanced placement needs, job reskilling, and many other niche areas.

Among the criticisms that have been aimed at MOOCs and open education during the past few years is the concern that only a small percent of those who enroll follow through to the end of the course in spite of the initial registration by tens of thousands of learners. Not everyone agrees that this is a problem, nor what should be done about it if it is a concern. New ideas about the engagement of those who actually show up for the initial weeks of the course have been suggested by Harvard and MIT researchers (edX, 2014), among others.

In addition to retention and engagement concerns, some raise concerns about accreditation and certification from participation in a MOOC (Young, 2015). Still others pose legitimate questions about the assessment of learning from a MOOC or from other forms of open education. As expected, there will be feedback and assessment concerns related to courses that have more than a couple dozen students, let alone thousands or even tens of thousands (Dale, 2014). Where is the evidence that those thousands enrolled in a MOOC have learned something from it? The same question can be raised of self-directed learners who extensively or more casually explore other forms of open education such as OCW and OER. And, just as importantly, who is willing to accept that evidence as proof of some competency or skill? Given such questions, some people are beginning to ponder the forms of assessment and representation of skills attained that would be sufficient and effective for potential employers to accept MOOC training and OER explorations as viable (Alraimi, Zo, & Ciganek, 2015; Hickey & Uttamchandani, in press; Sandeen, 2013).

These are just a few of the pressing issues that MOOCs and more open forms of education have brought about the past few years. New educational ideas and alternatives in this emerging field of MOOCs and open education seem to emerge on a weekly, and at times, daily, basis. Which ones will win out is difficult to tell (for an extended discussion of this topic, see Reynolds, Reeves, Lee, & Bonk, 2015a).

When it comes to the open education movement and new forms of learning delivery, we clearly remain seated in the "Wild Wild West" of learning. Bang; another idea related to MOOCs and open education is offered. Along the way, open education--like most educational innovations--has accumulated numerous proponents and opponents. With mounting debates on MOOCs and open education, it is time to pose substantive questions. For instance, what are the potential benefits, drawbacks, and obstacles for faculty members, instructional designers, and learning managers as well as their organizations and institutions engaged in developing and implementing MOOCs and OER across educational sectors, be they in the K-12 field or working with adult learners in higher education, corporate training, or government settings? In addition, as apparent in a seemingly endless array of research articles and news reports, probing questions continue to be asked about the sustainability and financial viability of most MOOCs and open educational resources. This special issue was designed to address many of these key concerns and issues.

THE POWER OF FOUR

Throughout the editorial process for this special issue, we did, indeed, ask many such questions. Oftentimes, in this wild and wooly age of online learning, we barely had time to reflect on solutions to one problem before a couple more issues would arise. For nearly two years now, we have teamed up to decipher the prevailing literature on MOOCs and open education as it was published. Each of us has had our perspectives on what is a significant project or finding. Not too surprisingly, such collaborations have been central to new discoveries and innovations since the start of the early days of computing.

To highlight this point, in his most recent book, *"The Innovators: How a Group of Hackers, Geniuses, and Geeks Created the Digital Revolution,"* Walter Isaacson (2014) provides a thrilling account of how the digital revolution came to be. As he illustrates in each enticing chapter of this book, when one probes deeply into the monumental advancements in computing technology during the past two centuries, it is clear that timely innovation and creative sparks of genius did not suddenly emerge from highly secluded or hermit-like situations. Solitary pursuits were not the common spark for creative insight. Instead, innovation was more often the result of collaboration and the pooling together of an assortment of advances and incremental steps. Isaacson notes that it is the ability to work in teams that often allows for people to display creativity or mold something unique into existence. For Isaacson (2014), "an invention, especially one as complex as a computer, usually comes not from an individual brainstorm, but from a collaboratively woven tapestry of creativity" (p. 84). In effect, Eureka moments may actually be more evolutionary than revolutionary.

In such partnerships, serendipitous and opportunistic partnerships are formed which enable something distinctive and valuable to develop and then be cultivated. For instance, in describing the partnership of Ada Lovelace and Charles Babbage, Isaacson (2014) argued that it led to a famous scientific publication back in 1843. This translated article in *Scientific Memoirs* includes a series of notes by Ada Lovelace which are, in effect, what many deem to be the first computer program. Some 100 years later, during the 1940s, J. Presper Eckert and John Mauchly built what is considered the first modern computer, the ENIAC. A similar partnership was formed when Paul Allen and Bill Gates spent their free time and many late nights practicing coding during middle school, high school, and college in the late 1960s and far into the 1970s. And so it is with many of the ideas found in this special journal issue as well the events that led to it. As you will discover, several unique partnerships were formed in the writing of the articles that appear in this special issue.

Of the seven other pieces that appear here in addition to this preface, six involve teams of two. In his book, *"Powers of Two: Finding the Essence of Innovation in Creative Pairs,"* Joshua Wolfe Shenk (2014) uses rich storytelling to highlight the power of pairs of individuals to push each other to new heights, often by sparking creative insight and bringing about something novel or unique. He suggests that there are six common stages of these creative and highly productive teams, including: (1) the conditions that led to their initial meetings, (2) the forming of their joint identity, (3) the taking up of distinct and enmeshed roles, (4) finding an optimal distance and space to cultivate distinct ideas and experiences, (5) the ability to strike a balance between competition and cooperation of the pairs, and (6) the final phase of interruption when they lose that balance and the team is driven apart (Latson, 2014). In explaining these phases, Shenk discusses the pairing of Pablo Picasso and Henri Matisse, Steve Jobs and Steve Wozniak, James Watson and Francis Crick, John Lennon and Paul McCartney, and myriad other such creative pairs. Like Isaacson's (2014) gripping *"The Innovators"* book, as well as his biography of Steve Jobs before it (Isaacson, 2011), the series of stories in *"The Powers of Two"* combine to tell a valuable tale about the types of processes and partnerships that lead to creative insight, valuable product inventions, and new forms of artistry.

Sometimes, however, the most productive teams are larger than two. Such is also the case of this special issue. We, the team of four editors for this special issue on "MOOCs and Open Education" for the *International Journal on E-Learning (IJEL)*, have collaborated on a series of projects for more than seven years now. On Monday October 21, 2013, the four of us (Curt Bonk from Indiana University, Mimi Lee from the University of Houston, Tom Reynolds from National University, and Tom Reeves from the University of Georgia), coordinated a special one-day preconference symposium focused on *"MOOCs and Open Education around the World."* The event was held at E-Learn 2013 in Las Vegas and was sponsored by the Association for the Advancement of Computing in Education (AACE). The response was quite positive, as over 100 people attended the symposium. The final result of this event is this special journal issue as well as an edited book published by Routledge (Bonk, Lee, Reeves, & Reynolds, 2015a).

The story of our collaborative efforts began earlier than 2013, however. Five years prior, in fact, we organized a preconference symposium at the same conference and in the same city, but on a different topic; namely, E-Learning in Asia. Interestingly, that symposium also resulted in a special journal issue that was simultaneously made available as a print-on-demand book (Bonk, Lee, & Reynolds, 2009). At that time, we were a team of three—Curt Bonk, Mimi Lee, and Tom Reynolds. Unexpectedly, Professor Tom Reeves from the University of Georgia appeared at the gathering and asked to help out. In the end, he wrote the capstone piece to that special journal issue and book (Reeves, 2009) and recapped the day's events at the symposium. It was akin to one of those magical moments in life when the fourth member of a group appears just when needed (i.e., it was our Ringo Starr moment).

There is just something to be said for what teams of four people can accomplish that teams of two or three cannot. To recap, since 2008, we have run two successful preconference symposia, edited two special issues of this journal (one of which became a book; see Bonk, Lee, & Reynolds, 2009a, 2009b), and edited a comprehensive book (Bonk et al., 2015a). We have also helped organize the annual International E-Learn Conference run by AACE and create a new conference called Global Learn.

Our collaboration has been a rich and exhilarating experience. We have learned much together including a vast array of information about e-learning practices in Asia as well as how MOOCs and OER are being accepted and implemented today in many corners of the world. Editing this special journal issue is a case in point—we garnered new insights into the field of MOOCs from each round of editing and review. There is much happening each day in this space. Accordingly, as you will discover, some of it in the pages to follow.

OUR SEARCH INTO MOOCS AND OPEN EDUCATION

As we explored the literature on MOOCs and open education during the past few years, it was apparent that e-learning continues to proliferate globally, though in the United States, the pace of growth has begun to level off (Allen & Seaman, 2015; Kelley 2015). We also became aware that minimal attention has been placed on how individual regions of the world and particular countries are taking advantage of technology-enabled learning such as MOOCs. The possibilities for transformational change in developing and underdeveloped countries is widely accepted, but we had to ask ourselves, what is the reality? There is also an implied acceptance that e-learning, including MOOCs, is impacting young as well as older learners around the planet. But is this actually supported by evidence?

The four of us were aware that the emergence of new forms of blended learning (Horn & Stacker, 2015; Staker & colleagues, 2011, Staker & Horn, 2012) as well as the arrival of MOOCs and other forms of OER have made e-learning front page news across all continents and societies. When planning the preconference symposium, MOOCs, in particular, were repeatedly praised by the news media (Pappano, 2012) and yet were coming under increasing scrutiny (Dale, 2014; Hollands & Tirthali, 2014). With the preconference symposium, book, and this special issue, we sought to document what was indeed happening in various parts of the world as well as in different educational sectors and across different types of learners.

Given the proliferation of new digital forms of informal and formal learning, the four of us became aware of the increasing need to better understand how people in various regions of the world were implementing MOOCs and OER. As we read the waves of news reports and research studies (e.g., Gasevic, Kovanovic, Joksimovic, & Siemens, 2014; MOOC Research, 2014), we realized that educators, researchers, politicians, and countless others wanted to grasp what the outcomes of these initiatives are and how they can be improved. What also became clear to us is that MOOCs and MOOC-like derivatives as well as open education resources, projects, and initiatives have caused institutions and organizations to grapple with seemingly never-ending issues--such as those related to instructor roles in teaching a massive class (see article from Sarah Haavind and Cynthia Sistek-Chandler (this issue), accreditation and credentialing for those who complete it, quality standards of the content offered or embedded, innovative forms of assessment, and learner motivation and attrition.

In response to the above issues and other concerns, the preconference symposium that we held in October 2013 in Las Vegas explored and probed unique implementations of MOOCs and open education across regions and nations. The event also focused on the various opportunities as well as the dilemmas presented for these new forms of technology-enabled learning. As noted in the introductory article of this special issue by Mimi Lee and Tom Reynolds (see next article), the symposium participants spoke about their different delivery formats, the interaction possibilities that they witnessed, their unique grading schemes, and their current as well as projected business plans, among many other issues and concerns. Naturally, they also discussed the MOOC and open education trends in their respective locales. They also shared key research directions and findings and provided suggestions and recommendations for the near future. As such, it was quite a fascinating event.

Again, none of this would have been possible without extensive planning, thinking, discussion, and collaboration. As a team of four, we each had unique opportunities to think and share ideas about MOOCs and open education. We hope that you feel at least part of the experience the four of us went through during the past couple of years as you read through the articles in this special issue. We may not have been "massive" in our numbers, but we were certainly open and online throughout much of the process that led to this issue. Enjoy this one small take on MOOCs and open education as detailed in the articles of this special issue.

References

Allen, I. E., & Seaman, J. (2015). *2014 survey of online learning grade level: Tracking online education in the United States, 2014.* Online Learning Consortium (formerly the Sloan Consortium). Retrieved from http://www.onlinelearningsurvey.com/reports/gradelevel.pdf

Alraimi, K. M., Zo, H., & Ciganek, A. P. (2015). Understanding the MOOCs continuance: The role of openness and reputation. *Computers & Education, 80*, 28-38.

Belanger, Y., & Thornton, J. (2013, February 5). *Bioelectricity: A quantitative approach Duke University's first MOOC.* Duke University, North Carolina. Retrieved from http://dukespace.lib.duke.edu/dspace/handle/10161/6216.

Bonk, C. J. (2009). *The world is open: How Web technology is revolutionizing education.* San Francisco, CA: Jossey-Bass.

Bonk, C. J., Lee, M. M., & Reynolds, T. H. (Eds.) (2009a). *A special passage through Asia e-learning.* Chesapeake, VA: Association for the Advancement of Computing in Education.

Bonk, C. J., Lee, M. M., & Reynolds, T. H. (Eds.) (2009b). *International Journal on E-Learning, 8*(4). Special issue: A Special Passage through Asia E-Learning.

Bonk, C. J., Lee. M. M., Reeves, T. C., & Reynolds, T. H. (Eds) (2015a). *MOOCs and open education around the world.* New York: Routledge.

Bonk, C. J., Lee. M. M., Reeves, T. C., & Reynolds, T. H. (2015b). Preface: Actions leading to *"MOOCs and open education around the world."* In C. J. Bonk, M. M. Lee., T. C. Reeves, & T. H. Reynolds, T. H. (Eds.), MOOCs and open education around the world. NY: Routledge. Retrieved from http://publicationshare.com/moocsbook/

Bonk, C. J., Lee, M. M., Kou, X., Xu, S. & Sheu, F.-R. (2015). Understanding the Self-Directed Online Learning Preferences, Goals, Achievements, and Challenges of MIT OpenCourseWare Subscribers. Educational Technology and Society, 18(2), 349-368. Retrieved from http://www.ifets.info/journals/18_2/26.pdf

Carson, S. (2009). The unwalled garden: Growth of the OpenCourseWare Consortium, 2001-2008. *Open Learning, 24*(1). Retrieved from http://tofp.org/resume/Unwalled_Garden.pdf

Caswell, T., Henson, S., Jensen, M., & Wiley, D. (2008). Open educational resources: Enabling universal education. *International Review of Research in Open and Distance Learning, 9*(1). Retrieved from http://www.irrodl.org/index.php/irrodl/article/viewFile/469/1009

Christensen, G., Steinmetz, A., Alcorn, B., Bennett, A., & Woods, D. (2013, November 6). *The MOOC phenomenon: Who takes massive open online courses and why?* University of Pennsylvania. Retrieved from http://papers.ssrn.com/sol3/papers.cfm?abstract_id=2350964

de los Arcos, B., Farrow, R., Perryman, L.-A., Pitt, R., & Weller, M. (2014, November). *OER evidence Report 2013-2014: Building understanding of open education. OER Research Hub.* The Open University (OU) Institute of Educational Technology. Retrieved from http://oerresearchhub.files.wordpress.com/2014/11/oerrh-evidence-report-2014.pdf

Drake, M. (2014, February 9). Old school rules! Wisdom of massive open online courses now in doubt. *The Washington Times.* Retrieved from http://www.washingtontimes.com/news/2014/feb/9/big-plan-on-campus-is-dropping-out/?page=all

edX (2014, January 21). Harvard and MIT release working papers on open online courses. *edX Blog.* Retrieved from https://www.edx.org/blog/harvard-mit-release-working-papers-open#.VOEnbo1TFjs

FTI Consulting. (2015). *U.S. postsecondary faculty in 2015: Diversity in people, goals and methods, but focused on students.* Retrieved from http://postsecondary.gatesfoundation.org/wp-content/uploads/2015/02/US-Postsecondary-Faculty-in-2015.pdf

Gasevic, D., Kovanovic, V., Joksimovic, S., & Siemens, G. (2014). Where is research on massive open online courses headed? A data analysis of the MOOC Research Initiative. *The International Review of Research in Open and Distance Learning, 15*(5). Retrieved from http://www.irrodl.org/index.php/irrodl/article/viewFile/1954/3111

Hickey, D. T., & Uttamchandani, S. (in press). Beyond hype, hyperbole, myths, and paradoxes: Scaling up participatory learning in a big open online course, In E. Losh (Ed.). *The MOOC moment: Experiments in scale and access in higher education.* Chicago, IL: The University of Chicago Press.

Hollands, F. M., & Tirthali, D. (2014). *MOOCs: Expectations and reality.* New York: Center for Benefit-Cost Studies of Education, Teachers College, Columbia University. Retrieved from: http://www.academicpartnerships.com/sites/default/files/MOOCs_Expectations_and_Reality.pdf

Horn, M., & Stacker, H. (2015). *Blended: Using disruptive innovation to improve schools.* San Francisco: Jossey-Bass.

Isaacson, W. (2011). *Steve Jobs.* New York: Simon & Schuster.

Isaacson, W. (2014). *The innovators: How a group of hackers, geniuses, and geeks created the digital revolution.* New York: Simon & Schuster.

Kelly, R. (2015, February 5). Online enrollment growth slows, but still outpaces brick-and-mortar. *Campus Technology.* Retrieved from http://campustechnology.com/articles/2015/02/05/online-enrollment-growth-slows-but-still-outpaces-brick-and-mortar.aspx

Latson, J. (2014, August 27). 'Powers of two' by Joshua Wolf Shenk. *The Boston Globe.* Retrieved from http://www.bostonglobe.com/arts/books/2014/08/26/review-powers-two-joshua-wolf-shenk/MlV7IY0Kr4SgMnenujAyEK/story.html

Laurillard, D. (December 30, 2014). A*natomy of a MOOC for teacher CPD.* University College London, Institute of Education. Retrieved from http://www.lkl.ac.uk/cms/files/jce/reports/anatomy_of_a_mooc_for_teacher_cpd_ucl-ioe.pdf

MIT News (2001, April 4). *MIT to make nearly all course materials available free on the World Wide Web.* MIT: Cambridge, MA. Retrieved from http://web.mit.edu/newsoffice/2001/ocw.html

MIT Press Release (2007, November 28). *MIT Marks OpenCourseWare Milestone.* November 2007 Newsletter. Retrieved from http://ocw.mit.edu/about/media-coverage/press-releases/milestone/

MOOC @ Edinburgh 2013 – Report #1 (2013). *MOOC @ Edinburgh 2013 – Report #1.* University of Edinburgh, Edinburgh, Scotland. Retrieved from https://www.era.lib.ed.ac.uk/bitstream/handle/1842/6683/Edinburgh_MOOCs_Report2013_no1.pdf?sequence=1&isAllowed=y

MOOC Research. (2014). *Welcome to the MOOC research hub.* Retrieved from http://www.moocresearch.com/

Pappano, L. (2012, November 2). The year of the MOOC. *The New York Times.* Retrieved from http://www.nytimes.com/2012/11/04/education/edlife/massive-open-online-courses-are-multiplying-at-a-rapid-pace.html?pagewanted=all&_r=0

Reeves, T. C. (2009). E-Learning in Asia: Just as good is not good enough. *International Journal on E-Learning, 8*(4), 577-585.

Reynolds, T. H., Reeves, T. C., Lee, M. M., & Bonk, C. J. (in press). Open options: Recapping this book with eyes on the future. In C. J. Bonk, M. M. Lee., T. C. Reeves, & T. H. Reynolds, T. H. (Eds.), *MOOCs and Open Education Around the World.* NY: Routledge.

Sandeen, C. (2013). Integrating MOOCS into traditional higher education: The emerging "MOOC 3.0" Era. *Change: The Magazine of Higher Learning, 45*(6), 34-39.

Shenk, J. W. (2014). *Powers of two: Finding the essence of innovation in creative pairs.* Boston: Houghton Mifflin Harcourt.

Staker, H., & colleagues (2011, May). *The rise of K-12 blended learning: Profiles of emerging models.* Innosight Institute. Retrieved from http://www.innosightinstitute.org/innosight/wp-content/uploads/2011/05/The-Rise-of-K-12-Blended-Learning.pdf

Staker, H., & Horn, M. B. (2012, May). *Classifying K-12 blended learning,* Innosight Institute. Retrieved from http://www.innosightinstitute.org/innosight/wp-content/uploads/2012/05/Classifying-K-12-blended-learning2.pdf

Young, J. R. (2015, February 11). Meet the new, self-appointed MOOC accreditors: Google and Instagram. *The Chronicle of Higher Education.* Retrieved from http://chronicle.com/blogs/wiredcampus/meet-the-new-self-appointed-mooc-accreditors-google-and-instagram/55807

ABOUT THE EDITORS

Curtis J. Bonk is Professor of Instructional Systems Technology at Indiana University and President of CourseShare. Drawing on his background as a corporate controller, CPA, educational psychologist, and instructional technologist, Bonk offers unique insights into the intersection of business, education, psychology, and technology. A well-known authority on emerging technologies for learning, Bonk reflects on his speaking experiences around the world in his popular blog, TravelinEdMan. In 2014, he was named the recipient of the Mildred B. and Charles A. Wedemeyer Award for Outstanding Practitioner in Distance Education. He has also authored several widely used technology books, including *The World Is Open, Empowering Online Learning, The Handbook of Blended Learning, Electronic Collaborators*, and, most recently, *Adding Some TEC-VARIETY* which is free as an eBook (http://tec-variety.com/). He may be contacted at cjbonk@indiana.edu.

Mimi Miyoung Lee is Associate Professor in the Department of Curriculum and Instruction at University of Houston. She received her Ph.D. in Instructional Systems Technology from Indiana University at Bloomington in 2004. Her research interests include global and multicultural education, theories of identity formation, sociological examination of online communities, issues of representation, and critical ethnography. Mimi has published research on STEM related online teacher education, cross-cultural training research, interactive videoconferencing, opencourseware, and qualitative research. She may be contacted at mlee7@uh.edu.

Thomas H. Reynolds is currently a professor of Teacher Education at National University in La Jolla, California where he researches the design of online learning environments, standards-based online assessment, and innovations in e-learning. Before coming to National University, he served on faculty at Texas A&M University after earning earned his Ph.D. in Curriculum and Instruction at the University of Wisconsin-Madison. He has twice served as a Fulbright Scholar—2010 in Colombia where he researched open education resources and 1998 in Peru where he lectured on Web-based learning and technology-enhanced instruction. Present activities and responsibilities include projects in Colombia, coordination of an e-teaching and learning master's degree specialization as well as leadership in online quality assurance and online course review and development for National University. He can be contacted at treynold@nu.edu.

Thomas C. Reeves, Professor Emeritus of Learning, Design, and Technology at The University of Georgia, has designed and evaluated numerous interactive learning programs. In 2003, he received the AACE Fellowship Award, in 2010 he was made an ASCILITE Fellow, and in 2013 he received the AECT David H. Jonassen Excellence in Research Award. His books include *Interactive Learning Systems Evaluation* (with John Hedberg), *A Guide to Authentic E-Learning* (with Jan Herrington and Ron Oliver), and *Conducting Educational Design Research* (with Susan McKenney). His research interests include evaluation, authentic tasks for learning, educational design research, and educational technology in developing countries. He can be reached at treeves@uga.edu.

International Jl. on E-Learning (2015) **14**(3) Special Issue, 279-288

MOOCs and Open Education:
The Unique Symposium That Led to This Special Issue

MIMI MIYOUNG LEE
University of Houston, USA
mlee7@uh.edu

THOMAS H. REYNOLDS
National University, USA
treynold@nu.edu

The foundation for this special issue came about during an E-Learn preconference symposium on *"MOOCs and Open Education Around the World"* held prior to the International E-Learn Conference in Las Vegas in October 2013. That symposium engaged over 100 e-learning scholars from across the globe in a day-long conversation on the merits, methods, and future of massive open online courses (MOOCs) and open education. As detailed in this article, there was extensive dialogue and sharing of resources throughout the symposium event. Topics of discussion included instructor roles, credentialing, evaluation and assessment, learner issues such as retention and self-directed learning, administration and management, quality standards, quality, future trends, and so on. Conversations that day also resulted in several collaborative teams that produced the research presented in this special journal issue. As evidenced by the six articles that follow, those initial dialogues matured and now contribute to what is known and speculated about MOOCs and OER.

INTRODUCTION

The four co-editors of this special issue carried out a series of online meetings in the early part of 2013 to discuss what was then conceptualized as a preconference symposium proposal on open educational resources and its current poster child, MOOCs. Six months later, in the fall of 2013, the four of us served as the co-chairs of an AACE E-Learn one-day preconference symposium entitled *"MOOCs and Open Education Around the World."* The symposium focused on current opportunities and dilemmas that MOOCs and open education bring to 21st century learning, with specific attention paid to MOOC design and delivery, MOOC demographics, MOOC licensure and credentialing, and the impact of MOOCs on current higher education leadership and faculty, especially business models and faculty roles and responsibilities. Aside from these content goals, like other event planners, the four of us wanted the symposium to not only result in useful dialogue and idea sharing, but we also hoped that it would foster community and ongoing collaborations. As such, in an effort to establish social presence in advance of the event, we invited participants to do a short video introduction using Flipgrid technology as well as complete a short online survey, which the team then used to refine event themes and schedules.

THE FORMAT AND THE OUTCOME OF THE PRECONFERENCE SYMPOSIUM

The preconference symposium began with invited presentations in a brief and lively TED-talk style. The morning keynote speaker, Paul Kim from Stanford University, started off with his experiences related to offering MOOCs. In his keynote presentation entitled "MOOCs through the Lens of Sustainability," Kim pointed to the paradigm shift brought on by the recent MOOCs phenomenon and the questions that it has generated. For example, how do you differentiate a MOOC from a non-MOOC? Is it a MOOC if it is not massive? Is it still a MOOC if it is not open?

To make his point, Kim told the story of his 2012 MOOC course, "Designing a New Learning Environment" (DNLE) that attracted nearly 20,000 students. In DNLE, some of the students took on leadership roles and helped other class members by creating a glossary for all of the course materials. In effect, this project-based learning course was intended to promote skills needed in the twenty-first century such as systematic design and virtual collaboration skills.

In terms of sustainability, Kim presented two MOOC models: one through monetizing and another through passion. Kim pointed out that the recent popularity of YouTube made it possible for "anyone to become a teacher on anything" and that such innovations are producing a new generation of "edupreneurs." Another way to achieve sustainability is through passion that serves as "fuel for sustainability." Accordingly, Kim shared several inspiring stories of his former MOOC students who went on to devote themselves to serving underprivileged groups around the world, in part, as a result of their participation in his 2012 MOOC course. In the end, his DNLE MOOC certainly was a paradigm changing experience for many participants. But will the next generation of MOOC providers take his message to heart and be able to replicate, build on, and extend such paradigm changing approaches and experiences?

Following the opening keynote presentation, the attendees were encouraged to establish thematic groups based on their interests and then start discussions in targeted break-out table sessions. Participants discussed MOOC and open education trends in their respective locales, shared key research directions and findings, and provided suggestions and recommendations for the near future. Symposium facilitators monitored and fostered participant exchange of ideas within the various ad hoc discussion and sharing groups. For the discussions, which were initiated in the last two hours of the morning session, and then carried on through a working lunch and reported on during an afternoon report-out session, participants were presented with substantive MOOC and open education issues to stimulate and develop discussions such as: (1) What are the major MOOC and Open Education issues around the world?; (2) What are the new and exciting developments?; (3) What still needs to be developed?; and (4) Are there any research gaps in terms of accreditation, assessment, design, instructor role, content quality, learner motivation, etc.?

Table discussions were only semi-structured in order for the working sessions to be driven by participant interests and experiences. During this collaborative effort, participants self-grouped by areas of interest. The coordinators of the preconference symposium attempted to build in participant choice and customization where possible. As such, possible topics for each table were constructed based on the online survey, mentioned earlier, that was completed by those who signed up for the preconference. These topics included credentialing policies, learner issues (e.g., motivation, attrition, and retention), instructor roles, informal and self-directed learning, international degrees and partnerships, administration and management, quality standards, mobile and ubiquitous learning delivery, emerging technology tools, global and cultural factors, research and development, future trends and visions, etc. The participant survey prior to the conference helped to pre-determine the groups and their members, but, nevertheless, symposium participants were allowed to select any group to join. The thematic groups were coordinated by one or more designated session leader(s). In addition, the four symposium coordinators participated in one or more groups as observers, facilitators, or participants, depending on the particular group needs.

Given the immediacy and intensity of the group discussions, it was clear that the preconference survey was effective in soliciting participant interests as well as in providing a stimulus for discussion and social interchange. The diversity of opinions and wealth of expertise and experience situated around the table that formed on "instructor roles," for instance, enabled that large group to engage many high level discussions at that initial morning meeting as well as throughout the day. While there was not a preset list of questions or issues to discuss in each group, the symposium coordinators asked the groups to discuss some of the key controversies, challenges, and issues as well as the recent news and research findings related to their topic. Members pondered the open issues and questions related to their topic. What were the evaluation needs, research gaps, or design possibilities that no one seems to have targeted? Key points and issues for each group were recorded for each team. Later on at lunch, most teams continued their discussions, some of which were quite passionate.

The afternoon session, which was moderated by Tom Reynolds (National University), began with an expert panel comprised of the following participants: Karen Head (Georgia Institute of Technology), Melinda Bandalaria (University of the Philippines Open University), Mimi Lee (University of Houston), Paul Kim (Stanford University), Theo J. Bastiaens (Fernuniversität in Hagen, Germany and Open University, The Netherlands), and Tom Reeves (University of Georgia). The panel was asked to share their expertise on MOOCs and open education on the following three major issues: (1) attrition, (2) accreditation, and (3) assessment. For each issue, the following pointers and questions were given to the panel:

1. **Attrition:** One of the big criticisms about MOOCs is a high attrition rate of 90 percent or more in many courses offered by for-profit as well as non-profit organizations such as Coursera, edX, and Udacity. Is this really a problem in light of the fact that the courses are free and attract tens of thousands of enrollees in many cases? And if it is a problem, what should be done about it?

2. **Accreditation**: Traditional education programs and institutions undergo some form of formal accreditation process that warrants that the degrees issued by them have some value. MOOCs and OER for the most part are not accredited at this time. Are the existing accreditation procedures even relevant in the context of open education? If not, what alternative mechanisms are needed to provide evidence of the quality of open educational learning environments?

3. **Assessment:** Weak assessment is frequently listed as a major limitation of various forms of open education. What evidence do current assessment practices provide that students and members of the general

public are achieving meaningful learning outcomes through engagement with MOOCs/OER in higher and/or K-12 education? And if the evidence is weak, how can more reliable and valid assessments of learning outcomes be accomplished?

4. **Alternative Assessment/Credentialing:** Salman Khan from the Khan Academy is among a number of innovators seeking to move away from traditional higher education degrees to a system of "micro-certifications" that would clearly demonstrate the competencies attained by learners through open education. What are the benefits, drawbacks, and obstacles in moving away from a credit/course-based degree model and moving toward a competency-based credentialing system?

In addition to the above targeted questions the following themes emerged out of the panel discussion:

1. **Design Issues:** Tom Reeves and others on the panel made it very clear that MOOC design is a critical e-learning issue, to say the least. However, as noted by both Tom Reeves and Melinda Bandalaria, most MOOC design does not reflect current thinking or competence in the field of instructional technology and instructional design when compared to what many hold as requisite for 21st learning and teaching standards. In effect, there is much that the fields of instructional technology and instructional design can offer to MOOCs and open education as free and open forms of education continue to emerge as a significant form of delivering instruction.

2. **Competency and Credentialing Issues:** Tom Reynolds and others on the panel supported the notion that MOOC accreditation, credentialing, badging, and certifying are also critical e-learning issues. In fact, several audience questions (from North American and African countries) targeted this area. Fortunately, as Tom Reynolds noted, there are many extant (i.e., existing and available) online learning examples of how to assess competence and assure that the competencies are aligned with professional society standards, standards of practice, and institutional or governmental criteria via identification and verification that there is close alignment between (for example): 1. ILOs (Institutional Learning Outcomes), 2. PLOs (Program Learning Outcomes), and 3. CLOs (Course Learning Outcomes), among others. Such assessments should also align learning experiences and competencies to workplace skills—teacher education being one noted example where standards of practice as well as governmental criteria require close adherence to such alignment and verification.

3. **MOOCs and Business Models:** Theo Bastiaens effectively argued that MOOCs, at their present stage of development, are an over-hyped innovation wherein the vast majority of the students do not perform and even fewer complete. His comments were clearly backed by the research and popular media related to this new form of educational delivery. In addition, he noted that there were presently no business models (or even instructional frameworks) for profitable MOOC management. This issue is especially pertinent when universities are faced with increasing challenges in the form of standards to meet, mounting budgetary cutbacks and shortfalls, rising societal expectations, etc. As such, from Bastiaens' perspective, it is highly problematic to invest precious time, money, and effort into innovations that are not part of current operations of a college or university, as present resources are increasingly constrained. Bastiaens' point is well taken when one considers that an institution like San Diego State University receives some 50,000 applications each fall semester but only has openings for 10% of them. Given the paucity of viable MOOC business models, these concerns are not easily assuaged.

4. **Personal Experiences:** The panel participants discussed the MOOCs that they had designed, taught, enrolled in, or browsed. For instance, Melinda Bandalaria spoke about the MOOCs that she was helping to design at University of Philippines Open University. In addition, Karen Head reflected on the MOOC that she recently taught and instructional issues surrounding it (e.g., feedback, learner diversity, the localization of content, assessment, etc.). At the same time, Tom Reeves discussed MOOCs that he both took as a learner as well as one that he had helped to teach with people from the UK, while pointing to various problems and difficulties in instructional design.

After the expert panel, the participants returned to the self-selected groups and continued with their discussions from the morning session. While groups were encouraged to create an action plan or establish an action agenda of next steps (e.g., a poster of key points, a model or framework, a potential research project or set of projects, a special journal issue, a cross-cultural collaboration plan, etc.), the actual format of these discussions and ultimate goal was left to each team. In the end, most of the groups chose to conduct roundtable discussions about engaging in benchmarking or brainstorming solutions to various challenges that, in some cases, led to exploring future plans for collaborative research or program development.

Most of the groups seemed to have used the afternoon session to continue discussions on their respective topics of choice from the morning session. At the end of the afternoon discussion session, a short debriefing session was held where each team presented the outcomes of their break-out sessions. Team leaders provided short three to seven minute recaps of their discussions. More or less, all groups mentioned some issues related to assessment and evaluation in MOOCs, at times asking more fundamental questions regarding the changing roles of universities and even the difficulty of defining MOOCs.

Several special and quite interesting items came to the forefront in the group recap sessions. For instance, in terms of the assessment in MOOCs, the possibility of automated evaluation systems and the promotion of more peer-to-peer generated evaluation was mentioned by Sarah Haavind in her group presentation as an example of the potential for the "horizontality of instruction" as opposed to top-down verticality of traditional instructional situations. Ideas related to providing a sample spectrum of submissions for peer evaluation or rubrics that support peer-to-peer feedback were also suggested as ways to facilitate assessment. At the same time, the instructor's role was discussed in relation to learners' (often) unrealistic expectation of immediate feedback from instructors. Additional issues such as structured vs. non-structured courses and the scaffolding of assignments were also presented as topics for further investigation. Importantly, the group recap presentations were video recorded and saved for later viewing and analysis.

The afternoon keynote presentation was delivered remotely by George Siemens, a pioneer of the emerging learning perspective called "Connectivism" and a person commonly associated with founding cMOOCs. In defining knowledge as a pattern of connections, Siemens emphasized that innovation required openness for forming new connections. In the midst of all the current hype regarding MOOCs, Siemens demanded that our attention be directed to "online learning, the development of new software, new assessment techniques, and new pedagogies." Siemens concluded his talk by posing a "Where next?" question to the audience, encouraging continuous and active dialogues that explore the legacy of MOOCs in bringing forth change in higher education. The day ended with the preconference symposium coordinators' recapping events of the day.

INTRODUCING THE SPECIAL ISSUE

The preconference event was fortuitously sponsored by the Association for the Advancement of Computing in Education (AACE), which publishes the *International Journal on E-Learning (IJEL)*. Just prior to the event, the conference founder, Dr. Gary Marks, suggested that the four coordinators assemble a special issue of this journal on *"MOOCs and Open Education"* based on the preconference symposium. As a result, near the end of the day, a call for papers for the special issue of IJEL was announced and audience participation was solicited. Given the amount of energy and wealth of ideas displayed throughout the day, the special journal issue would serve as a means to extend and share the communal energy of the event by putting it into a sharable product. A reminder email about the special issue was sent out to participants shortly after the event terminated and proposals were then submitted and reviewed. During the next six months, articles for this special issue went through several rounds of review and revision, with about half of the initial proposals making it to completion for this issue. On the whole, the interactive and collegial spirit of the symposium carried forward throughout the review process.

As the backbone of this special issue, the next six articles provide an in-depth look at various topics regarding MOOCs and open education. For instance, in the first article titled, "Peer2Peer and Open Pedagogy in MOOCs to Support the Knowledge Commons," Helene Fournier and Rita Kop explore a possible solution to prevailing assessment questions and issues. It is vital to point out that we start this volume with this particular article since it provides an historical overview of the evolution of MOOCs as well as key aspects of research and development related to MOOCs to date. Particularly salient in the article from Fournier and Kop is research on connectivist MOOCs (i.e., cMOOCs) and the processes, tools, and features that make cMOOCs function effectively. Importantly, this piece also explores some of the recent as well as upcoming research and development efforts that are being undertaken in a new Learning and Performance Support System (LPSS) program at the National Research Council (NRC) in Canada. In effect, in this lead article, the authors provide both critical base knowledge as to the current status of MOOCs and open education as well as an extended glance at the possibilities for tomorrow.

Following that initial piece is Ke Zhang's comparison of three MOOC communities in China using big data. Her paper, "Mining Data from Weibo to WeChat: A Comparative Case Study of MOOC Communities on Social Media in China," explores an especially timely topic given the recently exploding academic and government interests in data mining. The data for this study were derived from prevailing social media that currently is expanding in use in China. Zhang's research results indicate that when MOOC communities are leveraged through social media, they can find success for those in rural and remote areas of China. She ends with a highly useful list of 15 strategies that, according to her research, appear to contribute to the success of MOOC communities in China. As such, those interested in the state of MOOCs in China are well advised to read this article and perhaps put into practice some of her timely ideas and recommendations.

As in any instructional setting, high quality teachers are the crucial component of effective learning. The massiveness of MOOCs, by their nature, necessarily demand a quality instructor for their success. In this regard, it is important how we understand the rapidly modifying roles of instructors brought about by MOOCs and open education. To that end, the authors of the next article, Sarah Haavind and Cynthia Sistek-Chandler, directly respond to this issue in their paper titled "Role Play: Emergent Role of the Instructor in MOOCs." In this qualitative case study, Haavind and Sistek-Chandler interviewed eight instructors who taught different types of MOOCs including xMOOCs, cMOOCs, and various types of MOOC hybrids. Instructional practices that they explored include personalization, fostering student-centered instruction, feedback, strong content, and various managerial and presentation skills. As might be expected, across the eight cases, they found that for any instructor considering offering a MOOC, a major challenge is developing a course that provides an optimal combination or balance between delivering the contents and addressing the needs of the users of it (i.e., the learners).

In the fourth article Shoba Bandi-Rao and Christopher Devers present an in-depth look at the development of MOOC courses for remedial writing. They propose that MOOCs can play a significant role in preparing students at community colleges for academic life, thereby increasing their odds of completing their degrees. Bandi-Rao and Devers detail five types of MOOCs that might better address the needs of remedial writers, many of which are similar to those discovered by Haavind and Sistek-Chandler in the previous article. The authors' argue that of most importance for remedial writers is personalized feedback and support. As such, they review how each type of MOOC that they describe can enable such individually tailored guidance.

In emphasizing the importance of continuous self-reflection on MOOCs, the following article by Vicki Williams and Nai-Fen Su of Pennsylvania State University provides a critical review of current MOOC research, especially in terms of the effectiveness of MOOCs. In this paper, "Much aMOOC about Nothing: Is Real Research Coming?," Williams and Su offer interesting tables related to the types of MOOC publications (e.g., dissertations, government publications, conference papers, newspaper stories, scholarly journal articles, working papers, etc.). Of particular importance, the authors document that MOOC research is definitely on the rise. They also conclude with guiding questions for future research on MOOCs such as how instructors can elicit higher levels of thinking in MOOC courses. In the end, they appropriately point out that the data indicate that the field of MOOCs is currently beginning to blossom. Suffice to say, those reading this special issue with the goal of knowing more about the state of the research on MOOCs will find many important clues in this article.

Those exploring the final article of this special issue of IJEL will notice that the two other editors for this special issue, Tom Reeves and Curt Bonk, detail key variables related to the quality of MOOCs and open education. More specifically, in their article, "MOOCs: Redirecting the Quest for Quality Higher Education for All," Reeves and Bonk provide a highly insightful review of different rubrics, models, and dimensions of quality that might be considered in MOOC development and evaluation. In their quest for quality, they advocate for design based research approaches that can elevate MOOC and open education standards behind all-too-common bare minimums. They also offer some final comments and insights on the preconference symposium as well as this special issue. While they remain optimistic about the potential for MOOCs and open education, they also explicitly point out that significant quality improvements are now needed for the MOOC and open education movement to push ahead.

Given the above contributions that emerged from one special day of intensive discussion on MOOCs and open education in October 2013, one can easily understand why the preconference symposium was considered a success. One of the key reasons for this sense of accomplishment was that there was an immediate sense of community and camaraderie generated among the participants. And, as noted, the fact that some of those participants went on to collaborate and share their conversations here in print attests to the viability of such endeavors. As such, not only was it a highly interactive day filled with intense and thought stimulating discussions, but this special issue continues that conversation, with several of the collaborative teams that formed during the conference contributing to it. In addition, several more attendee groups are continuing their discussions and research in different formats and venues. As you read this special issue, we hope that you will expand your own discussions and research collaborations related to MOOCs and open education or begin entirely new ones.

Mimi Miyoung Lee is Associate Professor in the Department of Curriculum and Instruction at University of Houston. She received her Ph.D. in Instructional Systems Technology from Indiana University at Bloomington. Her research interests include global and multicultural education, theories of identity formation, sociological examination of online communities, issues of representation, and critical ethnography. Mimi has published research on STEM related online teacher education, cross-cultural training research, interactive videoconferencing, opencourseware, and qualitative research. She may be contacted at mlee7@uh.edu.

Thomas H. Reynolds is currently a professor of Teacher Education at National University in La Jolla, California where he researches the design of online learning environments, standards-based online assessment, and innovations in e-learning. Before coming to National University, he served on faculty at Texas A&M University after earning earned his Ph.D. in Curriculum and Instruction at the University of Wisconsin-Madison. He has twice served as a Fulbright Scholar—2010 in Colombia where he researched open education resources and 1998 in Peru where he lectured on Web-based learning and technology-enhanced instruction. Present activities and responsibilities include projects in Colombia, coordination of an e-teaching and learning master's degree specialization as well as leadership in online quality assurance and online course review and development for National University. He can be contacted at treynold@nu.edu.

International Jl. on E-Learning (2015) **14**(3) Special Issue, 289-304

MOOC Learning Experience Design: Issues and Challenges

HÉLÈNE FOURNIER
National Research Council Canada
Helene.Fournier@nrc-cnrc.gc.ca

RITA KOP
Yorkville University, New Brunswick, Canada
rkop@yorkvilleu.ca

This paper will present current work on various frameworks that are aimed at guiding the research, development, and evaluation efforts around Massive Open Online Courses (MOOCs). Initiatives and activities, including current work by the National Research Council (NRC) in the context of Learning and Performance Support Systems and MOOCs, will be presented along with outstanding challenges and issues to be addressed in the near future. Findings from case studies of Personal Learning Environments (PLEs) and MOOCs will be presented which suggest that learning experiences are impacted by much more than tools and technologies. There is the potential for an enormous palette of possibilities for creating effective, meaningful, and successful learning experiences, as well as many important issues and challenges to address. Recommendations coming of out of recent cMOOC surveys and forums will highlight participant focused and learner driven processes along with a changing notion of time and space in online learning environments. The paper also unveils current and future areas of research and development in a new Learning and Performance Support System (LPSS) program at NRC, including learning analytics, big data, and educational data mining, as well as ethics and privacy issues in networked environments and the use of personal learning data to feed into the research and development process.

INTRODUCTION

The term MOOC (Massive Open Online Course) was coined in 2008 by George Siemens (University of Texas Arlington) and Dave Cormier (UPEI) who facilitated their first online course with hundreds of participants distributed geographically, while the content, communication and collaboration were hosted by a large variety of social media platforms.

Initially MOOCs were based on connectivist principles and supported by emerging technologies which facilitated peer to peer interaction and made it possible to collaborate and share resources on an unimaginable scale. The topic of this first cMOOC was "Connectivism and Connective Knowledge" (CCK08) (Downes, 2008, 2011).

MOOCs have since added to the range of online learning options and are considered to be a disruptive educational trend, especially in Higher Education and lifelong learning (Hyman, 2012; Yuan & Powell, 2013). A range of both topics and platforms have since emerged and the term MOOC has been described as "the educational buzzword of 2012" by Daniel (2012) reflecting widespread interest in the concept. In 2012, Brooks referred to the hyperbole surrounding the rollout of MOOCs as a "campus tsunami" that was purportedly poised to change the face of higher education.

Amidst all the hype are what seem to be two sound rationales for the existence of MOOCs. The first one relates to their potential for extending learning opportunities for those who would not otherwise have them. And the second one concerns the possible enhancement of the quality of learning and teaching. Interestingly, while much of the positive feedback has focused on the noble sentiments behind making world-class courses (mostly from elite universities) freely available to anyone located anywhere in the world, a fair amount of the negative press aimed specifically at instructionist MOOCs or xMOOCs has revolved around the quality of the courses themselves (Daniel, 2012). The criticisms run the gamut of instructional design issues surrounding MOOCs; however, dropout and low completion numbers have garnered the most attention. These last two criticisms may be misplaced as they are founded on historical assumptions about learning environments and outcomes that do not necessarily apply to the recent phenomenon of MOOCs, at least not without some reconsideration and reframing (Grover, Franz, Schneider, & Pea, 2013). Hersch and Merrow (2005) suggest that beyond the learning opportunities MOOCs extend to learners around the globe REAL (Research, Evaluation, Assessment for Learning) strategies around MOOCs must be maximized in order to avoid recreating some of the same substandard, weak, and inadequate designs of higher education instruction of today (as cited in Reeves & Hedberg, 2014, p. 7).

This paper will present current work on various frameworks that are aimed at guiding the research, development, and evaluation efforts surrounding MOOCs. Various other initiatives and activities around MOOCs, including current work by the National Research Council in the context of Learning and Performance Support Systems and MOOCs will also be presented along with outstanding challenges and issues to be addressed in the near future.

MOOC FRAMEWORKS

MOOC research, development, and evaluation

In order to strengthen the efforts around MOOCs, various frameworks have been proposed for research, development, and evaluation, and for the design of more effective MOOCs, to maximize their potential impact on the existing educational sector. Grover, Franz, Schneider, and Pea (2013) have proposed a design and evaluation framework for MOOCs (Figure 1) based on distributed intelligence that encompasses the social and material dimensions, as well as the traditional roles and responsibilities of teachers distributed among learners because of the scale of the MOOC. The framework proposes specific as well as interrelated features that should work together in order to foster personal as well as cooperative learning.

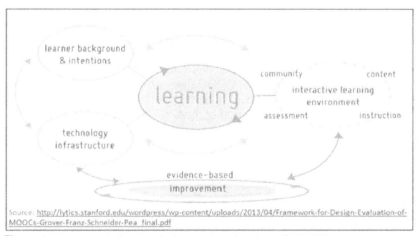

Source: http://lytics.stanford.edu/wordpress/wp-content/uploads/2013/04/Framework-for-Design-Evaluation-of-MOOCs-Grover-Franz-Schneider-Pea_final.pdf

Figure 1. Framework for the design and evaluation of MOOCs.

While the interactive learning environment is at the heart of the learning experience, this framework emphasizes that it is the interaction between the learning of individual participants and the collective learning that result in deeper learning experiences. The expertise of all participants in the development of the environment, such as instructional designers, faculty, technologists, and data analysts, contributes to shaping the environment for optimal learning. This framework (Figure 1) for the design and evaluation of MOOCs shifts the focus of responsibility from the learning institution and faculty members towards a form of participatory learning for the MOOC participants as a whole. Built into the framework are elements of design for innovative and previously untested technology infrastructure elements such as scaffolding for the formation of social learning groups, peer assessment, question-clustering techniques, polling or voting mechanisms, or an automated system that provides "feel good" rewards or "karma points" (see Lewin, 2012) as an incentive to support learning by others in the MOOC.

In order to help guide conversations and advance notions of design, research, and evaluation of MOOCs even further, a new framework for MOOCs in higher education was proposed as part of the MOOC Research Initiative, led by George Siemens at University of Texas Arlington and funded by the Bill & Melinda Gates foundation. An asynchronous, typed, online discussion (also referred to as a Jam) was organized by George Siemens in November of 2013. This session brought together experts in online learning to discuss and design a new framework for MOOCs in higher education. The invitation-only MOOCJam generated much discussion aimed at bringing about order and institutional alignment on the topic of MOOCs, along with consistency and agreement on standards (Mackness, 2013). The Jam discussion, which was intended as a peer review forum, focused on the design of the framework, including a review of its strengths and weaknesses, structural integrity, and the selection, organization, and comprehensiveness of elements. This new MOOC framework (Figure 2) was informed by the ELLI profile, or Effective Lifelong Learning Inventory, which was developed over a three year period at the University of Bristol, resulting in several strands of knowledge. Mackness (2013) has argued that efforts to develop a framework for MOOCs may go against what MOOCs are trying to promote—that is openness, interactivity, diversity, and autonomy. By fitting MOOCs within a framework, the potential for experimentation and promoting creativity and innovation in Higher Education may be compromised.

Mackness (2013) argues that the purpose of a framework for MOOCs must be clear and remain true to the initial aspirations of the early MOOCs; that of being disruptive to Higher Education in searching for new ways to think about and democratize education. Other important components of the MOOC Jam framework (Figure 2) include the learner profiles, assessments, and support required for learners in the environment, which should all be considered as existing on a continuum. Research efforts related to personal learning environments and MOOCs have also contributed important baseline information on learning experiences beyond the tools and technologies. The next section presents important research findings from these various efforts.

George Siemens introduces a new MOOC Framework

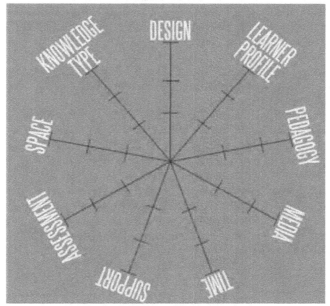

Figure 2. Framework for MOOCs.

Research on personal learning environments

The National Research Council Canada (NRC) has been conducting research on MOOCs since 2009 and has also proposed a framework for conducting research in the area of Personal Learning Environments (PLEs), including MOOCs as a particular instance of PLE (Kop & Fournier, 2013b). The ultimate aim of this work is to help online learners in the context of

PLEs to work more effectively but also to contribute to a higher level of engagement and learning—along with efforts to develop support systems or components including: a profiler, aggregator, editor, scaffolds, and services. Previous PLE research and evaluation efforts (Fournier, Kop & Durand, 2014; Kop & Fournier, 2010, 2013a) have provided important baseline data about user experiences with existing tools, applications, systems, and desirable features for creating new and improved personal learning environments, including learning in the context of MOOCs.

The importance of human factors such as motivation, incentives, support (organizational, social networks, either online or in the community) in creating high-quality learning experiences have been highlighted. Findings from NRC case studies of PLEs and MOOCs have also suggested that learning experiences are impacted by much more than tools and technologies. Philosophical, ethical, contextual, and pedagogical issues surrounding the use of technologies on an individual level and in relation to others inside and outside the social network determine how people learn. The potential exists for an enormous palette of possibilities for creating effective, meaningful, and successful experiences.

A great deal is already known about various experiences and their creation through established disciplines that can - and must - be used to develop new solutions. According to Shedroff, "most technological experiences—including digital and especially, online experiences—have paled in comparison to real-world experiences and have been relatively unsuccessful as a result. What these solutions require first and foremost is an understanding by their developers of what makes a good experience; then to translate these principles, as well as possible, into the desired media without the technology dictating the form of the experience" (Shedroff, 2009, p. 3). It is imperative to not let the technology dictate the development.

Recently, the NRC collaborated on the research and development of an International French MOOC on the topic of Open Educational Resources (OERs); a course lasting nine weeks, with 1,273 participants registered, from geographically dispersed locations across the globe—see CLOM REL 2014 at http://rel2014.mooc.ca/. Online surveys were conducted as part of ongoing information gathering efforts to feed into evolving cMOOC design and development work. Participation in three surveys administrated across the course included representation from Europe (60%), Africa (25%), and America (15%).

A conscious effort was made in the learning design of the MOOC to incorporate structures that might alleviate some of the challenges experienced by cMOOC participants in earlier MOOCs. A collaborative design was adopted with open tools and pedagogy combining both a directive approach (xMOOC type), focused on content, with a networked learning approach of a connectivist type (cMOOCs). The project was developed in an open mode with the following technical implementation: (1) gRSShopper platform to host content and aggregate the contributions of participants and their discussions, (2) the media for publishing chosen by the participants which also serve as their portfolio, usually a blog, and (3) social media adopted for the course either the Google community, Twitter, and a Facebook page.

The course platform, that is the gRSShopper personal Web environment, provided a place to view course content, to participate in the course by viewing the daily newsletter, the ability to view and post comments in discussion forums, options to view calendars of live events and recorded sessions, as well as sharing RSS feeds. The gRSShopper application would then aggregate content from all feeds with the course hashtag #CLOM REL 2014, including posts and comments to forums and to personal blogs.

Information on new course content and updates was published in a daily newsletter that was emailed to participants who had subscribed to the newsletter service. In addition, the course Web environment would provide daily updates. The course relied heavily on video and text, both updated on a weekly basis, including a video introduction to the week's topic by an expert, various resources and activities, and recordings of live hangout sessions with the experts. Survey comments indicated that there were connectivity issues for those participating in certain parts of Africa, therefore accessing video content was problematic. Offering low-tech options to access content, in PDF file format for example, should be considered in the MOOC design where connectivity may be an issue; this is now part of the lessons learnt for MOOCs offered worldwide.

Essentially, following this first delivery of the OER MOOC, a foundation of solid contributions and capacity building for (French) open educational resources was laid. Currently, interested parties not only can direct their members to specific sections of the course and the course content, but also adapt their own teaching approach combined with the content available. This is referred to as a "wrapped" approach to online learning or MOOC design which consists of utilizing free and validated pedagogical approaches and content to organize one's own set of learning activities around a topic of interest and around the expertise available.

The recommendations coming out of this recent cMOOC derived from surveys and forum discussions include: (1) the need for assessing the impact of the OER MOOC, (2) the desirability of disseminating shorter timely courses for specific participants (who may be more receptive to these specific events), (3) the need to operationalize (one or more specific aspects of) the adoption of OER by specific communities of interest, (4) the need to identify the core workflow for operationalizing OER, and, as in previous MOOC studies and lessons learned, participants indicated (5) the need to develop an accreditation mechanism that is open for continuing education relating to OERs. As Dave Cormier, our facilitator for Week 8 of the OER MOOC pointed out (Figure 3), in addition to the phenomenon of peripheral participation in cMOOCs, there is also a participant driven process whereby the course continues on even after it has officially ended.

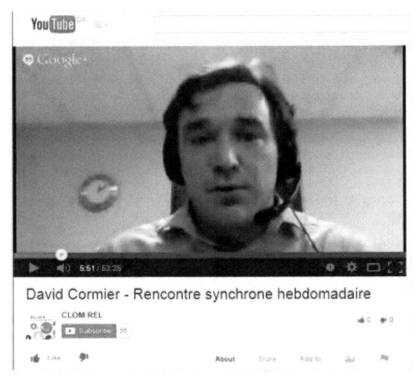

Figure 3. French recorded hangout session-accessible from https://www.youtube.com/watch?v=pC9yH7mUHx0.

The notion of a participant driven process underscores the changing notion of time and space in MOOCs as well. In the Rhizo14 MOOC (also referred to as #rhizo 14) participants continued the course without a teacher filling the role as guide or decision maker, for another 6 weeks, with activity in the Facebook, Twitter, and the Google+ realm, and the communal learning process continuing on. People posted ideas, challenges, and thoughts and others brought their perspective to it, and learnt often in vastly different ways, from each interaction (Cormier, 2014).

Similarly, a recent Stanford University MOOC (Coursera's Machine Learning Course—the third offering—ML3) introduced badges for the first time and had about 60% of the students registered before the class officially began and another 18% registered after it ended. This implies that a significant number of the students are interacting with courses solely after they end, which is an unexpected way in which MOOCs differ from traditional classes (Anderson, Huttenlocher, Kleinberg, & Leskovec, 2014). This difference in course content duration and learner activity was also the case for the OER MOOC, as discussions and newsletter contributions continued to flow after the course had officially ended, with participants and experts alike contributing to possible next steps for French-community capacity building of OERs. Such behaviour suggests that MOOC participants perceive MOOCs to be different from a traditional course; more as a learning event with open access Web-resources contributing to a community of learners or learning commons.

Despite the wealth of information now available on MOOCs through various scientific publications and social media including blogs, microblogs, wikis, and social networks, there is no shortage of challenges and issues to be addressed. The next section will highlight some of the obvious ones.

MOOC Learning Experience Design

Challenges related to learning and experience

To date, research on cMOOCs has pointed to the conditions that clearly encourage the involvement and engagement of people in learning in a connectivist learning environment, including: (1) the social presence of the facilitators and of participants, (2) feeling competent and confident in using the different tools, (3) learning in an autonomous fashion without the provision of organized guidance by facilitators, and (4) the emergence of critical literacies such as collaboration, creativity, and a flexible mindset, which are prerequisite for active learning in a changing and complex learning environment (Kop, 2011).

Empirical research into the actual MOOC experience is still sparse and areas of particular weakness include information on the types of support systems required by learners to be successful in MOOCs. There is also an overreliance on metrics commonly used in education to measure success in MOOCs, namely the number of enrollments, completion rates, and assessments. Accreditation and engagement continue to pose a challenge in MOOCs—whether in dealing with the semantics of digital badges, automated grading, calibrated peer review, learning analytics for assessment and adaptive learning, distance proctoring, and engagement diagnosis and remediation (Alain, 2014). Individuals now need a wide range of competencies—social skills, communication, problem solving—in order to face the complex challenges of today's world; especially those related to this increasingly digital world.

Important challenges remain to be addressed in order to ensure quality MOOC learning experience design. Current efforts to address important challenges related to personalization, ethics, and the use of personal learning data will be presented in the following sections.

Challenges related to personalization and supporting individual learning needs

Efforts directed towards "mass customization" are currently aimed at restructuring MOOCs at the individual level and to personalize information, resources, and communication in order to best support each student, and not only the aggregate (Salvador, De Holan, & Piller, 2009). These efforts also tie into the persistent challenge of sustained and personal engagement across both xMOOCs and cMOOCs. Participants in cMOOCs continue to express the need for greater presence of course facilitators, which makes cultivating a relationship with the course instructor or tutor a real challenge given the large number of students to attend to. To this end, Coursera has recommended an approach that borders in part on course automation, that is, a computer assigns classmates to give one another feedback. However, automated feedback does not provide students with a sense of being treated as an individual, and, therefore, falls short in providing personalized learning.

Additional inroads are also needed to begin to understand the specific types of resources that informal learners find valuable to their changing learning needs. Further insights into the purposes and goals leading someone to use a specific OER over another or to sign up for a particular MOOC are needed. The factors or learning components which support participant retention in a MOOC are still not well understood nor are the online supports or scaffolds that can be embedded to increase weak completion numbers of most MOOCs to date (Catropa, cited in Bonk 2013). Comments received in the OER MOOC surveys underscore similarities between the barriers or challenges in MOOCs and many self-directed learning environments, which include less immediate feedback and guidance, lack of personalization, procrastination, and becoming overwhelmed by the resources made available (Graham, 2006). Increasingly, information about individual learners and their online behaviors are made available and harvested from their participation in MOOCs. Researchers need to carefully consider the ethical implications related to how personal learning data is collected, analyzed, and reported.

Challenges related to ethics and the use of personal learning data

Researchers need to consider the ethical implications of the chosen methods of obtaining data for a study as well as the use of the data. Johnson (2014) writes about the ethics of big data in higher education and the problems of privacy and individuality. According to Kitchin (2014, p.1), "The challenge of analyzing Big Data is coping with abundance, exhaustivity and variety, timeliness and dynamism, messiness and uncertainty, high relationality, and the fact that much of them are generated with no specific question in mind or are a by-product of another activity." The use of learner data to enhance future learning has created a debate around the ethical use of data gathered from online learners. The recent Facebook experiment on emotional contagion (Authur, 2014) and a call from academics for clear guidelines to prevent the misuse of personal information (Schreurs, de Laat, Teplovs, & Voogd, 2014) both serve to highlight the debate and issues around informed consent in conducting research which could potentially influence or affect users' social media. Clearly, the issues are broad and complex.

CONCLUSION

It has been suggested that the proliferation of MOOCs in higher education requires a concerted and urgent research agenda. A body of research has started to develop. For instance, the MOOC Research Initiative (MRI) has made an effort to address research gaps by evaluating MOOCs and how they impact teaching, learning, and education in general (http://www.moocresearch.com/announcing-mooc-research-initiative).

Researchers have access to massive amounts of data that capture the entire digital experience in a constant stream of inputs and outputs, but the challenge is the effective analysis of such big data. It is easy for researchers to resort to the easiest way of capturing quantitative data, which would leave out the richness that more qualitative efforts could achieve. Some efforts are being made to develop data-driven learning environments that include features for visualizing traces of data that learners have left behind in their online learning activities (Downes, 2013; Duval, 2011). Machine-learning techniques to personalize the learning experience are also being pursued (Spice, 2014).

Social learning analytic tools are being applied in MOOC environments to stimulate, monitor, and evaluate networked learning activities. Tools such as the Network Awareness Tool (NAT) plug-in increases the power of analytics such that participant can render their connected world more visible. Visualizing networked learning activities can help learners to decide which discussion topics they should join and which experts they should aim to connect with (Schreurs, de Laat, Teplovs, & Voogd, 2014). Among the major complaints from participants in the recent French OER MOOC was the challenge of sifting through threaded discussions to find relevant contributions, an overabundance of discussions and content, and the difficulty of knowing who contributed what, especially in one's area of interest or learning. Tools for visualizing networked learning activities could help in supporting learners in MOOCs. Still, with MOOC learning analytics there are the challenges of going beyond the logs, observing and making sense of interactions, annotations for assessment, dynamic adaptation of learning processes, the need to provide avenues for deeper learning, while managing and protecting the identity and privacy of learners (Alain, 2014). Moreover, there are also difficult issues relating to identity fraud, plagiarism, peer learning, meaningful feedback, and assessment of learning outcomes which need to be addressed going forward.

Two major threads of our work at NRC over the last few years have been MOOCs and Personal Learning Environments. The gRSShopper project and our PLE prototype development both included research and development of cMOOCs in the context of a network theory of learning, and now feed into the research and development of a new Learning and Performance Support System (LPSS) program at NRC. This program explores the challenges of personal learning and performance support, including areas of focus such as learning analytics, big data and educational data mining, and ethics and privacy issues in networked environments and the use of personal learning data feeding into the research and development process. It also looks at agile methodologies for improving system design and efficiency as well as implementing open badges and credentialing mechanisms. The goal of LPSS is to create a single point of access to all skills development and training needs, with individual learning paths, context-aware support, searchable and verifiable skills and competency records, and tailoring to industry needs as required. This research will inform the next generation of learning design, which includes a combination of machine-learning, analytics, and human interactions.

Systems — be they techno-social systems, course recommender systems or learning and performance support systems — must be effective, carefully crafted and designed to promote learner autonomy along with REAL (Research, Evaluation, Assessment for Learning) strategies (Hersch & Merrow, in Reeves & Hedberg, 2014). The LPSS program has already put important mechanisms in place in its research and development environment to start addressing the challenges and issues of personal learning and performance support, including an internal research ethics review of the collection and use of personal learning data feeding into the research and development process. With the advent of social media and opportunities to connect people on a massive scale, we have now entered a new era of communication and trust. Learners, participants, and consumers of technologies should be encouraged to make informed decisions about what they share, who they share with, and what might be the potential risks and benefits in contributing and participating. Transparency as well as sound data privacy, security, and trust practices by those producing new technologies and learning environments are now a priority.

References

Alain, M. (2014). *MOOCs: New research questions and method?* Retrieved from http://prezi.com/owhcvtpwsu5q/moocs-new-research-questions-and-method/

Anderson, A., Huttenlocher, D., Kleinberg, J., & Leskovec, J. (2014). Engaging with massive online courses. Engaging with massive online courses. *Proceedings of the 23rd International Conference on the World Wide Web*, 687-698. doi:10.1145/2566486.2568042. Retrieved from http://arxiv.org/pdf/1403.3100.pdf

Authur, C. (June, 2014). Facebook emotion study breached ethical guidelines, researchers say. *The Guardian*. Retrieved from http://www.theguardian.com/technology/2014/jun/30/facebook-emotion-study-breached-ethical-guidelines-researchers-say

Bonk, C. J., Lee, M. M., & Sheu, F.-R. (2014). Research on self-directed informal learners in open educational environments and massively open online courses. *Presented at AECT, Anaheim on November 1 2014*. Retrieved from http://trainingshare.worldisopen.com/pdfs/Self-Directed_Lrng_MOOCs_Open_Ed_AECT_Bonk_et_al_Friday_paper_session--Title-Change.pdf

Brooks, D. (2012, May 3). The campus tsunami. *New York Times*. Retrieved from http://nyti.ms/SJ4vl0.

Cormier, D. (2014). Community learning—the zombie resurrection. *Dave's Educational Blog: Education, post-structuralism and the rise of the machines*. Retrieved from http://davecormier.com/edblog/2014/05/25/community-learning-the-zombie-resurrection/

Daniel, J. (2012). Making sense of MOOCs: Musings in a maze of myth, paradox and possibility. *Journal of Interactive Media in Education, 3*. Retrieved from http://www-jime.open.ac.uk/jime/article/viewArticle/2012-18/html

Downes, S. (2008). Places to go: Connectivism & connective knowledge. *Innovate: Journal of Online Education, 5*(1). Retrieved from http://bsili.3csn.org/files/2010/06/Places_to_Go-__Connectivism__Connective_Knowledge.pdf

Downes, S. (2011, November 20). MOOCs and the OPAL (Open Education Quality Initiative). *Quality Clearinghouse*. Retrieved from http://www.downes.ca/post/57770

Downes, S. (2013, December 4). Learning and performance support systems. *Half an Hour blogspot*. Retrieved from http://halfanhour.blogspot.com.es/2013/12/learning-and-performance-support-systems.html

Duval, E. (2011). Attention please! Learning analytics for visualization and recommendation. *Proceedings of 1st International Conference on Learning Analytics and Knowledge, February 2011*, Banff, Alberta, Canada.

Fournier, H., Kop, R., & Durand, G. (2014). Challenges to research in MOOCs. *Journal of Online Learning and Teaching, 10*(1). Retrieved from http://jolt.merlot.org/vol10no1/fournier_0314.pdf

Graham, C. R. (2006). *Blended learning systems: Definition, current trends, future directions*. In C. J. Bonk and C. R. Graham (Eds.), The handbook of blended learning: Global perspectives, local designs (pp. 3-21). San Francisco, CA: Pfeiffer Publishing.

Grover, S., Franz, P., Schneider, E., & Pea, R. (2013). The MOOC as distributed intelligence: Dimensions of a Framework & Evaluation of MOOCs. In *Proceedings of the 10th International Conference on Computer Supported Collaborative Learning, Madison, WI, June 16-19*. Retrieved from http://lytics.stanford.edu/wordpress/wp-content/uploads/2013/04/Framework-for-Design-Evaluation-of-MOOCs-Grover-Franz-Schneider-Pea_final.pdf

Hyman, P. (2012). In the year of disruptive education. *Communications of the ACM, 55*(12), 20-22.

Johnson, J. A. (2014). The ethics of big data in higher education. *International Review of Information Ethics, 7*, 4-9. Retrieve from http://www.i-r-i-e.net/inhalt/021/IRIE-021-Johnson.pdf

Kitchin, R. (2014). Big data, new epistemologies and paradigm shifts. *Big Data & Society, 1*(1). Retrieved from http://bds.sagepub.com/content/1/1/2053951714528481.full.pdf+html

Kop, R. (2011) The challenges to connectivist learning on open online networks: Learning experiences during a massive open online course. *The International Review of Research in Open and Distance Learning, 12*, 3. Retrieved from http://www.irrodl.org/index.php/irrodl/article/view/882/1823

Kop, R., & Fournier, H. (2010). New dimensions to self-directed learning in an open networked learning environment. *International Journal of Self-Directed Learning, 7*(2), 1-20. Retrieved from http://www.sdlglobal.com/IJSDL/IJSDL7.2-2010.pdf

Kop, R., & Fournier, H. (2013a). Social and Affective Presence to Achieve Quality Learning in MOOCs. In T. Bastiaens & G. Marks (Eds.), *Proceedings of World Conference on E-Learning in Corporate, Government, Healthcare, and Higher Education 2013*, 1977-1986. Chesapeake, VA: AACE.

Kop, R., & Fournier, H. (2013b). Developing a framework for research on personal learning environments. *eLearning Papers. Open Education Europa, No 35*, November 2013. Retrieve from http://www.openeducationeuropa.eu/sites/default/files/asset/In-depth_35_4.pdf

Lewin, T. (July 18 2012). Q&A with Anant Agarwal: One course, 150,000 students. *New York Times*. Retrieved from http://nyti.ms/MiZR5f

Mackness, J. (Nov 23 2013). Lassoing the coltish concepts of emergent learning and MOOCs. *Jennymackness.wordpress.com*. Retrieved from http://jennymackness.wordpress.com/2013/11/23/lassoing-the-coltish-concepts-of-emergent-learning-and-moocs/

Reeves, T. C., & Hedberg, J. G. (2012). MOOCs: Let's get real. *Educational Technology, 54*(1), 3-8.

Schreurs, B., de Laat, M., Teplovs, C., & Voogd, S. (2014). Social learning analytics applied in MOOC-environment. *eLearning Papers . OpenEducationEuropa, 36*, 45-48. Retrieved from http://openeducationeuropa.eu/en/download/file/fid/33697

Salvador, F., De Holan, P. M., & Piller, F. (2009). Cracking the code of mass customization. *MIT SloanManagement Review, 50*(3). Retrieved from http://www.ie.edu/microsites/comunicacion/Sem%2018%20mayo%202009/Salvador,%20De%20Holan%20&%20Piller.pdf

Shedroff, N. (2009). Experience design 1.1: A manifesto for the design of experiences. *Experience Design Books*. Retrieved from www.experiencedesignbooks.com

Siemens, G. (2013). Peer review of a framework for MOOCs. Momentum.edthemes.org. *Introduction to the MOOCJam*. Retrieved from http://momentum.edthemes.org/about-mooc-jam/

Spice, B. (2014) Press release. Google sponsors Carnegie Mellon Research to improve effectiveness of online education. Paying attention to how people learn promises to enhance MOOCs. *Carnegie Mellon News*. Retrieved from http://bit.ly/1I6Ns0N

Yuan, L., Powell, S. (2013). MOOCs and disruptive innovation: Implications for Higher Education. *eLearning Papers, In-depth, 33*(2), 1-7. Retrieved from www.openeducationeuropa.eu/en/download/file/fid/27007

Hélène Fournier has been a Research Officer at the National Research Council Canada's Institute for Information Technology since 2002 and holds a Ph.D. in Educational Psychology from McGill University. Her research area is education and technology. She has participated in several research projects focused on the application and evaluation of advanced technologies in the training sector, in distance education, and more recently in learner-centered research and development of Connectivist Massive Open Online Courses (cMOOCs) and Learning and Performance Support Systems. Dr. Fournier has contributed to the advancement of research in the field of distance education, online learning, and adult learning. She has also been engaged in the study of informal learning experiences in the context of cMOOCs. She has published widely in peer reviewed journals and at international conferences. She can be contacted at Helene.Fournier@nrc-cnrc.gc.ca.

Rita Kop is dean of the Faculty of Education at Yorkville University, She has been a researcher at the National Research Council of Canada and holds a Ph.D. in Adult Continuing Education. Her current research focuses on human learning in advanced networked learning environments. Before she joined the NRC, she was an assistant professor at Swansea University in the UK. At Swansea, Dr. Kop worked with community groups and universities contributing to community-based and online services for adults in some of the most deprived areas of the UK. Dr. Kop is originally from the Netherlands, where she spent ten years as teacher and head teacher in elementary education. For more information: http://www.you-learn.org. She can be contacted at rkop@yorkvilleu.ca.

International Jl. on E-Learning (2015) **14**(3) Special Issue, 305-329

Mining Data from Weibo to WeChat:
A Comparative Case Study of MOOC Communities on Social Media in China

KE ZHANG
Wayne State University, MI, USA
ke.zhang@wayne.edu

This article starts with an overview on China's MOOC phenomenon and social media, and then reports a comparative, multiple case study on three selected MOOC communities that have emerged on social media in China. These representative MOOC communities included: (a) MOOC Academy, the largest MOOC community in China, (b) Zhejiang University of Technology MOOC Group, the first officially registered student MOOC organization in China's universities, and (c) a fully online community devoted for high school (or younger) students in MOOCs. Data were collected through a variety of Chinese social media (e.g., Sina Weibo, QQ Qun, and WeChat), social networking sites (e.g., Baidu Tieba, GuoKr, Sina blog, etc.), news press, and Web-based community portals. Text mining and content analyses were conducted to study the varied MOOC communities and how they functioned on social media to promote MOOCs as well as to support MOOC learners and the broader community. Implications for research and practice of MOOC communities are discussed.

MOOC IN CHINA: A BRIEF OVERVIEW

In Chinese, MOOC (i.e., massive open online course) is translated into "Mu Ke," partly based on the similar pronunciations, with "Mu" meaning "adore" and "Ke" meaning "courses." But MOOC is used more often than its Chinese translation on social media and mass media as well. Shortly after, "MOOCer," a new English word also spread widely and became frequently used in Chinese MOOC communities as a nickname for MOOC learners and enthusiasts. If the year 2012 was "the Year of the MOOC" in the United States (Pappano, 2012), the year 2013 certainly witnessed powerful breakthroughs in terms of China's MOOC initiatives.

Since that time, elite universities in China have been increasingly contributing to the worldwide MOOC phenomenon. In May 2013, China's prestigious universities, such as Tsinghua University, Peking University, University of Hong Kong, and Hong Kong University of Science and Technology joined edX as charter members. Soon after, other esteemed universities, such as Fudan University and Shanghai Jiaotong University, joined Coursera. In addition, based on the open source code of edX platform, Chinese entrepreneurs built Xuetang Zaixian (https://www.xuetangx.com, meaning Schools Online). Xuetang Zaixian is a Chinese Web portal providing course information in simplified Chinese. The help system allows users to personalize their search for MOOC resources and courses by MOOC platform, offering university, subject, level of difficulty, and current status (e.g., past, ongoing, upcoming, etc.). Xuetang Zaixian provides direct links to 123 edX MOOCs, and MOOCs offered in Mandarin by highly regarded Chinese universities as well.

As a result of robust government initiatives on the national level, iCourse (http://www.icourses.cn/home/), a Web portal, has been developed as part of the flagship project co-funded by the Ministry of Education and Ministry of Finance in China (Zhang, 2011; Zhang, Liang & Sang, 2013). iCourse initially was limited to selected premium online courseware (Zhang, 2011; Zhang, et al., 2013). Now it has been further expanded with a special channel for MOOC offered by Chinese universities at http://www.icourses.cn/imooc/. Many Chinese universities also offer MOOCs via the domestically developed MOOC portal at: http://www.icourse163.org/, which is a collaborative outcome between Coursera and China's leading internet company, NetEase (Bildner, 2013a).

While increasingly more native Chinese speakers are enrolled in MOOCs offered in English or other foreign languages from overseas universities, the language barriers, technical issues (e.g., the difficulty to access or stream lecture videos from YouTube or OER on Google, both of which are banned in China), and learning cultural differences (e.g., Zhang, Peng,

& Hung, 2009) added tremendous challenges for Chinese MOOCers. The extremely low completion rate in MOOCs (Agarwala, 2013; Parr, 2013), despite the arguable interpretations, reflects some of the challenges faced all MOOCers.

In efforts to help more Chinese-speaking MOOCers, multiple international partnerships were built among MOOC providers, universities, organizations, and leading social networking sites in China and overseas. For example, NetEase, a leading Internet company in China created a Coursera Zone tailored for Chinese-speaking MOOC learners through collaborative efforts with Coursera (Bildner, 2013a, 2013b). It is housed on NetEase' popular Web portal, 163.com (http://c.open.163.com/coursera/home.htm#/courseraHome). This Coursera Zone offers the following features and services in Chinese: (a) easy access to Coursera course descriptions in Chinese, (b) many Coursera course videos for streaming or downloading, which otherwise would not have been accessible because YouTube, the original hosting site, is banned in China, (c) FAQs, and (d) discussion forums in Chinese for MOOCers.

In one short year, MOOCs became extremely well received and many turned into hot topics on social media in China. For example, Peking University offered its well-liked course, "Flipping Classrooms" via iCourse163.org in summer 2014 (see http://www.icourse163.org/course/pku-21016#/info). This course was so popular that QQ Qun, a social media for free group communications via mobile devices or desktops, quickly reached its 2,000 membership capacity. Moreover, a second QQ Qun was also filled almost instantly once made available. Consequently, the server hosting the course was jammed with too many learners online at the same time which brought the course website down while it was ongoing. The teaching crew had to utilize multiple, additional, and alternative cloud services to facilitate large amounts of file sharing, video streaming, and downloading. The eventful MOOC became one of the hot topics on China's social media in the summer.

SOCIAL MEDIA IN CHINA

Even though most social media originated in the western countries are banned or otherwise not available in mainland China, domestically developed Chinese social media have been increasingly popular during the past few years. In fact, many of these social media have hundreds of millions of active users from China and overseas. Weibo, for example, is a microblogging tool in Chinese (often compared to Twitter) with 250 million users in 2011 (China Internet Network Information Center, 2013). QQ Qun, is another popular, free social media that facilitates group communications on mobile devices or desktops, with the option to be open or private, or, in effect, searchable or not searchable. Baidu Tieba (or Baidu Bar), the largest Chinese communication platform on the Web hosts tens of millions user-created "bars" (Web-based communities) with over 10 billion visits in 2010 (Zhou, 2010). Numerous communities have formed on these varied social media in China.

Research suggests that social media may play an active role in building and sustaining learning communities. For example, Reynol Junco and his colleagues (Junco, Heiberger, Loken, 2011) found that the microblogging enabled sustained discussions. As a result, it helped build a strong learning community amongst students beyond the formal learning boundaries. Similarly, Ebner and Maurer (2009) found increased sense of community and network building through the use of microblogging. Although researchers recognize the potential of social media in community-building, limited research has thoroughly examined those more open-ended informal communities, as opposed to learning communities created or mandated by instructors. In addition, little is known about how such informal learning communities function within social media.

With the increasing popularity of MOOCs in China, MOOC communities have emerged on Chinese social media sites. For instance, a recent study explored popular informal learning communities emerged on China's social media for science learning, and discovered the important roles social media played in informal science learning as well as community building (Zhang & Gao, 2014). There is scant research on MOOC communities either in China or elsewhere. This multi-case comparative case study explored three well-respected MOOC communities, each representing a different community of MOOCers in China. The following research questions were investigated:

- How do MOOC communities in China utilize social media to promote MOOC and to support MOOCers?
- How do different MOOC communities serve varied members?

RESEARCH DESIGN

As an empirical enquiry, the case study method allows in-depth investigation of a contemporary phenomenon within its real-life context (Yin, 2009). And, compared to single-case design, multiple-case design is typically more robust with a higher explanation power (Santos & Eisenhardt, 2004; Yin, 2009). Thus, in this study, three MOOC communities were carefully chosen and analyzed, following the general principles of case study research to build a deep understanding of popular and highly influential MOOC communities that have emerged on Chinese social media.

Data Sources and Data Collection Processes

Multiple datasets from various sources were collected to enhance data credibility (Patton, 1990; Yin, 2009), including archives of MOOC community Web space, ongoing social media channels these MOOC communities utilized, media reports and other secondary data, and learning artifacts when applicable. Examples of data collected from social media included Sina Weibo (e.g., tweets, re-tweets, comments or responses, etc.), Sina Blog, Baidu Tieba, Douban, QQ Qun, Community Web portal, user blogs, WeChat, and other social media sites as applicable (see Table 1).

Table 1
A summary of Data Sources and Types

Data Source	Data	Type of Data
Sina Weibo http://www.weibo.com/ URLs vary by UserID	• Tweets • retweets • comments • hashtags • hot topics • numbers of "thumbs up"	• textual • date and time • frequencies
Sina Weibo UserID profile URLs vary by UserID	• description • self-selected WeiQun (micro-communities) • number of followers	• textual • date and time • frequencies
Community Web portal	• communities • discussion boards • blogs • activities • user-generated content • Q&A • number of participants • hot topics	• textual • date and time • frequencies
Sina Blog http://blog.sina.com.cn URLs vary by UserID	• blog entries • comments	• textual • date • frequencies

Table 1 Continued

Data Source	Data	Type of Data
Baidu TieBa (Baidu Bar) http://tieba.baidu.com URLs vary by "bar"	• posts • comments • number of reads	• textual • date & times • frequencies
QQ Qun http://qun.qq.com (Login required & mostly accessed on mobile devices with password protection)	• QQ Qun membership information • types of community • QQ Qun descriptions	• numeric • categorical • textual
WeChat (see http://www.wechat.com/en/ for information)	• userID profile information • daily pushed messages on WeChat	• textual
Media Reports (e.g., Xinhua News, China Daily, iFeng.com, etc.)	• news reports • comments	• textual • dates

Data collection started before the three MOOC communities were selected, when the researcher actively followed multiple MOOC communities on social media both as a MOOCer and as a curious researcher. All social media data sources were followed on a daily basis from May to early August in 2014. In addition, ROST Content Mining system, Version 6.0 (Shen, 2011) was utilized during the primary research period for textual data mining (Hung & Zhang, 2008, 2012; Zhang & Gao, 2014) to search, identify, and extract relevant textual data from popular social media in China on MOOC or MuKe (the Chinese translation). ROST was selected as the text mining system in this study because of its well-recognized capacity for searching and extracting textual data in simplified Chinese and its customized features for analyzing Sina Weibo content (e.g., Zhang & Gao, 2014).

The three MOOC communities were identified and selected for further analyses by the end of May, and systemic data collection on these communities followed from June 1 to August 10, 2014. The researcher took reflective notes, both as a MOOCer and as a curious researcher. Researcher notes and reflective journals were constantly reviewed to guide and refine the focus of data analysis efforts.

MOOC Community Selection

Three MOOC communities were identified and selected for this in-depth, comparative case study, each representing a unique community of MOOCers in China. The selection process itself was part of the primary research inquiry, as the researcher learned "onsite" about the MOOC communities both as a user of Chinese social media and an active MOOC learner herself. The three MOOC communities chosen for further analyses were: (1) MOOC Academy, (2) Zhejiang University of Technology (ZUT) MOOC Group, and (3) High School MOOCer Bar. Firstly, the MOOC Academy (MA) was selected because it is the largest Chinese MOOC community and it hosts half of MOOCers in China on its social networking sites (MOOC Academy, 2014a). Next, the ZUT MOOC Group (ZUT.MG) was selected because it was the first officially registered student organization on MOOC in higher education institutions in China. Interestingly, this student-initiated organization has received strong support from ZUT officials since its establishment (Zhejiang University of Technology MOOC Group, 2014). Finally, the third community was High School MOOCer Bar (HS.MB), a completely online MOOC community devoted to high school students and younger MOOCers in China, with pre-teen MOOCers actively leading and serving the community.

DATA ANALYSES

All data were recorded, read, analyzed, and triangulated with both quantitative and qualitative methods (Creswell, 2003, 2005; Creswell & Clark, 2007). All textual data were read, coded, categorized, recoded, and then analyzed. In particular, content analyses were conducted to identify and categorize themes, such as:

- Types of Postings (e.g., blog entries, tweets, retweets, comments, forum messages, etc.)
- Types of Media (e.g., text, url, blog, video, web portal, graphics, photos, etc.)
- Community Contexts (e.g., Sina Weibo, Baidu Bar, QQ, WeChat, face-to-face, etc.)
- Membership boundaries (e.g., age, school grade, location, course, subject, profession, etc.)
- Support and help (e.g., seeking support, offer help, moral support, etc.)
- Motivation and Rewards (e.g., member recognition, self motivation, etc.)
- Artifacts (e.g., notes, written reflections, revised notes and learning reflections, concept maps, photos of assignments or creative activities, subtitle, translations, etc.)

Cases were initially constructed and analyzed individually, and cross-case themes were identified and critically analyzed afterwards to discover case similarities and differences.

FINDINGS

MOOC Communities on China's Social Media

During the initial explorative period of the study, through searches on popular social media sites as well as ROST searching and text mining processes, it was found that different social media tended to attract distinct types of MOOC communities. For example, QQ Qun (http://qun.qq.com), a free group communication social media for mobile devices, was particularly popular with course- or subject-specific MOOC communities (see Table 2).

Table 2
Most Popular MOOC Communities on QQ Qun
*As of Beijing Time 12 noon August 10, 2014

Name of MOOC Community	No. of Members*	Course-specific	Subject-specific	Geo-location based
iMOOC.com Fans Club	1421	No	No	No
Flipping Classrooms (multiple)	1,000 each	Yes	No	No
GuoKr MOOC Self Study Room (note: later became MOOC Academy)	999	No	No	No
Foundations of College Students Entrepreneurship	866	Yes	No	No
Chinese History	576	Yes	No	No
Psychology	356	No	Yes	No
Coursera_MOOC	320	No	No	No
Beijing MOOC Circus	242	No	No	Yes
MOOC	203	No	No	No
Computer Science MOOC Communications	190	No	Yes	No
Gamification	173	Yes	No	No
High School MOOCers	168	No	No	No

It is worth noting that even though there was only one geo-location based MOOC community (i.e., Beijing MOOC Circus) among the 13 most popular ones, there were indeed a lot more location-based MOOC communities on QQ Qun. Most of the location-based MOOC communities, however, had less than 100 members. Many of the MOOC communities on QQ Qun were password protected or otherwise set as private for member protection and to avoid spam or telemarketing.

While on Sina Weibo, MOOC communities were centered around organizational userIDs, such as MOOC offering institutions and MOOC platforms. On Web portals, MOOC communities were built in multiple ways, including the traditional threaded Web-based discussions, special interest groups, material sharing spaces, archived FAQs, and other features and functions.

MOOC Academy (MA)

MOOC Academy (MA) was founded by GuoKr.com, a highly successful science learning social networking site (Wang, Yao, & Ji, 2012; Zhang & Gao, 2014). In 2013, it was only a small virtual group devoted to MOOCs as part of GuoKr science learning communities (GuoKr, 2014a; Zhang & Gao, 2014). By the time of this study in mid-2014, it had attracted nearly half of the MOOCers in China as a virtual home (GuoKr). The exploration of MA sketches a big picture of MOOC communities in China.

With a new Web portal devoted for MOOC learning (http://mooc.guokr. com), MA also attracted 256,769 followers on Sina Weibo as of midnight August 10, 2014 Beijing time. The MA portal partnered with several MOOC platforms, including Coursera and edX from the USA, OpenLearning from Australia, FutureLearn from UK, iversity from Germany, and the domestically developed Xuetang Zaixian, and eWant from Taiwan. The MA portal provided designated virtual areas for discussions, special interest groups (SIGs), perspectives on MOOC, and Star Boards for MOOCers to showcase their MOOC certificates, MOOC learning outcomes, and peer support.

MA embraced a broad and diverse membership. More specifically, members of MA included individual MOOCers, MOOC instructors, MOOC providing institutions, partnered MOOC platforms, high tech companies, and international NGOs. Clearly, it served as a central hub for many MOOCers in China. As such, it often helped to promote and connect institutional or organizational MOOC communities. As a social media "product" of a commercial company (i.e., GuoKr.com), MA teamed up with MOOC providers, high tech companies, and MOOC advocating organizations to offer face-to-face events which connected MOOCers with famous MOOC instructors. In addition, it attempted to motivate MOOCers and MOOCer groups by providing scholarships for completing MOOCs with honor. As part of such efforts, MA also reported on outstanding MOOCers in its frequent MOOCer highlights on social media.

One of the highly regarded SIGs housed at MA was the voluntary group working on translation of course materials and the creation of Chinese subtitle for MOOC lecture videos in foreign languages. The Star Boards recognized community members for both their individual MOOC achievements (e.g., number of completed MOOCs, number of MOOC certificates, etc.) and their contributions to the community, including the quality of their shared course notes as well as the helpfulness of their posts and responses. Importantly, such recognitions were all based on member ratings.

MA On Sina Weibo

From June to August 10, 2014, MA posted a total of 637 tweets on Sina Weibo in 71 days, with an average of 9 or more tweets daily. able 3 summarizes the different types of MA tweets on Sina Weibo from June 1, 2014 to August 10, 2014. Most of these tweets on Sina Weibo were MOOC recommendations (n= 299, 46.9%) with a brief textual message on how the course may relate to one's personal or professional interests, or as related to current social events, or hot social topics. All MOOC recommendation tweets had multiple media components, always with a Web link to additional course information or directly to the MOOC offering website. The MOOC recommendation tweets each had a picture of the instructor and/or a video clip of course highlights. These tweets were frequently retweeted by MA community members or reposted later with a friendly, and often funny reminder.

Consistently, all motivation tweets (n= 49, 7.69%) were hash-tagged as #MOOC gentle whipping#. Such "gentle whipping" postings were written with a subtle touch of humor, or were related to an ongoing social event or a hot topic on social media. For example, in July 2014 during FIFA World Cup, MA posted the following tweet, quoting the world famous soccer player Miroslav Josef Klose, "It's not a shame to fall, it's a shame to just lie there" with a photo of the heroic super star and his quote in German (see Figure 1). With a huge soccer fan base in China, this tweet, posted at 11:58 pm on July 9, after a big win of the German National Team at the semifinal, was re-tweeted with comments for 168 times, received 157 "thumbs up," plus 20 more comments, all within hours.

Figure 1: Example of #MOOC Gentle Whipping# tweet: The Klose quote.

Table 3
Summary of MA Tweets on Sina Weibo*
*As of 11:59pm August 10, 2014 Beijing Time

Code	CR	Mo	NS	MH	IH	C4P	SchP	Sub	Q&A	AS	News
Definition	Course Recommendation	Motivation	Notes Sharing	MOOCer Highlight	Instructor Highlight	Call for participation	Scholarship	Subtitle & Subtitle group events	Questions and Answers	Assignment Showcase	MA in news
June	115	20	16	4	1	15	0	1	0	0	0
July	135	21	20	1	8	11	6	3	4	1	1
Aug. 1-10	49	8	7	14	15	15	17	19	66	22	22
Total: 637	299	49	43	19	24	41	23	23	70	23	23
%	46.9	7.69	6.75	2.98	3.77	6.4	3.6	3.6	11	3.6	3.6

MA reached out to its members and interacted with them in a few different activities on social medial. For example, tweets categorized as call for participation directly invited actions or reactions from MOOCers. From June to early August in 2014, MA posted 64 tweets and retweets, almost once daily, to invite participants for face-to-face events (e.g., meeting

MOOC instructors), MOOCer profile surveys, and MOOC Scholarship Competition. In addition, through MOOCer highlights (n=19, 2.98%) and instructor highlights (n=24, 3.77%), MA attempted to promote MOOC instructor's social presence, strengthen connections among peer MOOC learners, as well as between learners and instructors. A key purpose of such connections was to help members find meaningful bonds or relationships with fellow MOOCers as well as the (often famous) instructors offering the MOOC.

Despite the frequent tweets from MA official ID on Sina Weibo, the interactivity level, as indicated by the numbers of retweets, "thumbs up," or comments by individual MOOCers, was rather low. On Sina Weibo, MA's community building efforts were mostly one-way information dissemination. Instead of individual MOOCers, most retweets and comments were from organizational MOOC IDs, such as MOOC offering institutions, MOOC platforms, and advocating companies and organizations. So where did MOOC learners build their virtual community on MA?

MA Web Portal

Many MOOCers in China identified MA, particularly the MA Web portal (http://mooc.guokr.com) as their virtual home. On Sina Weibo, MA interacted mostly with MOOC-related organizations; while on MA Web portal, MOOCers were more visible and active with various user-initiated activities.

MA Web Portal was organized into three major sections, (1) Courses, (2) Discussions, and (3) News and Opinions. The "Courses" section was a searchable MOOC database organized by language, subject, platform, institution, and MOOCer rating. For each MOOC listed on MA Web Portal, MOOCers may find course descriptions and MOOCer comments. One can also discover MOOCers' ratings of the course in terms of knowledge, instructor involvement, interestingness of the course, course design, and course difficulty level. MOOCers also posted and shared their course notes in this section.

The Discussions Section was highly active with two types of themed discussions, (a) long-term, highlighted and promoted special topics or themes, which were closely monitored by designated volunteer groups, and (b) MOOCer-generated themes. The long-term special themes included: (a) what is a MOOC, (b) how to learn in a MOOC, (c) how to choose an appropriate MOOC, (d) FAQ for new MOOCers, (e) MOOCer stories, and (f) MOOC Subtitle special zone. For example, the Subtitle SIG initiated a theme of discussions for MOOCers to report any errors they might have caught on any MOOC videos. The subtitle volunteer team monitored this theme of discussions closely and gathered MOOCer-reported errors and suggestions to guide their constant efforts to revise and improve subtitles for MOOC videos in non-Chinese languages.

MOOCers also initiated discussions on a wide range of topics, such as finding peers taking the same MOOC, sharing or searching for MOOC notes, asking for help, recommending MOOCs, and organizing communities or learning groups on other social media (e.g., QQ Qun, WeChat, and Baidu Bar). Such discussions were mostly course-specific or subject-specific. The different topics of these discussions could involve from as little as a few participants to thousands. Most such discussions typically received responses shortly after the initial posting. The level of interactivity and number of individual MOOCer participants were much higher than on Sina Weibo.

The News and Opinions was another section MA utilized to communicate with MOOCers on MOOC-related news and updates, reports and reflections on MOOCs, MOOC instructors, MOOCer experiences, and other perspectives. MOOCers and members of MA community were active contributors of articles published in this section, and often posted comments and extended readings as related to the articles.

MA built a large MOOC community with a variety of resources and communication channels for members such as individual MOOCers, MOOC providing institutions, MOOC platforms, and other organizations. In this community, MA promoted MOOC and MOOCer highlights on Sina Weibo through frequent tweets, retweets, and comments. And, more importantly, it helped MOOCers and the broader MOOC community to communicate and support one another in multiple ways on the MA Web Portal.

Zhejiang University of Technology MOOC Group (ZUT.MG):

Zhejiang University of Technology (i.e., ZUT) MOOC Group was the first official college student organization that was solely devoted to MOOCs. Importantly, it had received strong and consistent support from the university officials from its inception. As a direct consequence, it has become a model for many college or university MOOC organizations in China. ZUT.MG was founded by three students at ZUT in October 2013, and officially registered as a university-level student organization in November 2013 which soon enlisted over 200 members. It is noteworthy that the founders were all diligent MOOCers, and had each completed multiple MOOCs with certificates.

ZUT.MG: Social Media Uses

ZUT.MG had an active organizational ID on Sina Weibo with over 2,400 followers since they opened it in August 2013. In addition to individual MOOCers, ZUT.MG's followers also included many other MOOC organizations (e.g., Chinese Universities MOOCs), MOOC course ID (e.g., Harvard ChinaX), ZUT students, faculty, and administrators. The types of tweets and retweets posted by ZUT.MG included mostly course recommendations (n= 48, 62%), news reports on ZUT.MG (n= 14, 18%), and other MOOC related events (n=18, 19%). Like MA, most of the interactions on Sina Weibo were with other MOOC organizations.

An official WeChat (see http://www.wechat.com/en/ for more information) ID was also active with daily posts pushed to subscribers. On WeChat,
ZUT.MG shared various reports and articles on MOOC, MOOC instructors,
MOOC platforms, MOOC organizations, and related topics and perspectives. ZUT.MG also utilized QQ Qun (see http://qun.qq.com for more information), with approximately 300 members (ZUT.MG, 2014), where members were able to interact with free text, audio, or video messages.

ZUT.MG also hosted a blog on Sina Weibo (at http://blog.sina.com.cn/s/
articlelist_3772439187_0_1.html). From September 2013 to August 11,
2014, it posted 18 blogs there, including 6 entries about the organization itself and its updates (33%), 2 on MOOCs in general (11%), 6 highlights of
MOOC instructors (33%), and 4 MOOC notes sharing (22%). The number
of reads of the blog entries were low, mostly less than 10. However, most
of these blog entries were also shared on Sina Weibo, WeChat or QQ Qun,
where followers received them automatically. As a result of such dual posting, they may have been read more widely on other social media.

ZUT.MG Activities

ZUT.MG grew up through a series of MOOC-related events. In November 2013, they worked on the translation of Harvard's famous MOOC,
ChinaX, through partnership with GuoKr.com. In December 2013, they collaborated with NetEase' Cloud Classroom (http://study.163.com/#/index) in
a university-wide MOOC Motivation event, together with the first College
Students MOOC Production Competition. ZUT.MG regularly organized
local events to help prepare college students for online MOOC learning.
These lectures and seminars covered a wide range of topics, such as registration on different MOOC platforms, MOOC selections, MOOC learning
strategies and tips, and much more. ZUT.MG also held weekly face-to-face
seminars where MOOCers participated in subject-specific discussions as related to selected MOOCs. Critical to the overall success, they were able to
involve well-known faculty and experts in the weekly seminars.

Each semester, ZUT.MG also prepared and circulated a selection of relevant MOOCs schedules, and sent out friendly reminders when MOOCs
were about to start. The semester MOOC schedules were shared on blog,
Sina Weibo, WeChat and QQ Qun. To help MOOCers overcome the English language barrier, ZUT.MG invited a famous professor of ESL, Mr.
Jinghua Guan for a campus seminar on learning English (ZUT.MG, 2014).
ZUT.MG also reached out to famous MOOC instructors, and arranged additional opportunities for ZUT MOOCers to interact with them online or in
local events (ZUT.MG). These sessions were often recorded and uploaded
to ChuanKe, a domestically developed Open Educational Resources (OER)
in China. Consequently, such recordings and archives became part of the increasing MOOC supportive resources for Chinese-speaking MOOCers.

Even though ZUT.MG was an organizational community, and, thus was location-based, it made impacts beyond the geographic or organizational boundaries. As a highly respected and cutting-edge model of college/university student MOOC organization, many peer institutions and organizations followed ZUT.MG in their own efforts to establish MOOC communities and promote MOOC learning. The impact of ZUT.MG was also seen in how other Chinese institutions facilitated their MOOC offerings once they were established.

High School MOOCer Bar (HS.MB)

High School MOOCer Bar was a unique MOOC community. It was highly focused to serve a special group of MOOCers in China--those were still high school students or even younger. It had clear membership boundaries, as repeatedly confirmed on its virtual home on Baidu Bar (see: http://tieba.baidu.com/f?kw=%B8%DF%D6%D0moocer). Originally, it was housed on QQ Qun with about 200 members. While QQ Qun worked really well facilitating different ways of communications among members (e.g., one-to-one, one-to more, or all-to-all, etc.), it had limited capacity in hosting larger groups and the communications and resources shared there were not easily accessible to the general public. Thus, the community leader keenly grasped the need to make the community, as well as its resources, more visible and more accessible to all. As a direct result, it began to migrate to Baidu Bar in summer 2014.

HS.MB: Social Media Uses

HS.MB built a virtual home for high school (or younger) MOOCers in China on Baidu Bar. At the same time, the designated QQ Qun, noted above, continued serving as a more secrete and private space for member communications. As of August 10, 2014, on Baidu, the High School MOOCer Bar (HS.MB) had 17 major themes of discussions, 316 original posts, and 68 registered members.

HS.MB had clear strategies for members to collaborate and cooperate in MOOC learning, given the fact that high school students in China carried an extremely heavy workload at school and typically had hectic schedules. For example, HS.MB encouraged members to form MOOC learning groups with different formats. The highly recommended grouping format was called social learning groups (SLG). In SLG, course content or topics were allocated to each member, who would take the lead on learning it and be responsible for teaching and tutoring the rest of the group on their designated topics. HS.MB suggested that SLG should have five or more members, with pre-determined times to meet online, share their learning experiences, and teach fellow group members. High school MOOCers formed many course- or subject- specific SLG on the designated HS.MB bar area. Another format of grouping was referred to as free-style learning groups (FsLG), where members decide how they might want to collaborate or support each other.

In any groups, SLG or FsLG, HS.MB asked each group to identify a group leader. If no one would volunteer to serve as the group leader, the community leadership could nominate volunteers from experienced MOOCers to help the group. In addition, HS.MB provided a wide range of supporting groups, named Resources Group, Subtitle Group, Q&A Group, and, in similarity to MA, a "Gentle Whipping" Group (for motivation). The Resources Group was responsible for searching, downloading, organizing MOOC materials and extended readings, and uploading them to cloud storage for community sharing. The Subtitle Group took charge of translation and updating subtitles of non-Chinese MOOC videos, and was led by a young girl who started her MOOC adventure as an elementary school student. Gentle Whipping Group offered different forms of motivation, reminders, and encouragement for all community members, with a strong sense of humor just like the MA tweets, with the same hash tag or subject line, "gentle whipping." All supporting groups were publicly recruited via social media and were all volunteer groups. The HS.MB also had a policy or procedure to ask one representative from each service group to join every learning group as a handy assistant.

These young MOOCers, as demonstrated by their online activities, were highly self-motivated, with a strong sense of self-regulation. Overall, they loved serving the broader community through volunteering in supporting groups. For example, when an inquiry was posted on HS.MB asking people to serve on the Resources Group, a member immediately responded, "oh no, I was not asked to join the resource group?! I'm here volunteering to join! (smiley face). " Some of the MOOC leaders were found incredibly young, and surprised many, even long-term community members (Huanzai, 2014). For example, Icy, a nickname of her Sina Weibo ID, had 11 MOOC certificates (as of August 10, 2014) and had served years as a core member on the Subtitle Group in the MOOC community. When her personal Weibo indicated she was turning 13 in August 2014, many followers and MOOCers were surprised. (Note: even though it may be considered public data, I chose not to post her Weibo UserID or real name here, and decided not to cite her personal tweets on Weibo due to respect and protection of her as a minor user of social media.)

The HS.MB was the only community that sometimes were questioned or challenged by non-members as to whether or not young students (in high school or younger) should take MOOCs. The conversations often involved both HS.MB registered members, guests, other MOOC community members (such as MA members), and the high-profile MOOCer being questioned. Such interactive conversations led to in-depth discussions on the true value of MOOCs and their profound impacts on China's various educational systems, not only on higher education but also on K-12 and beyond. Such conversations became vital digital footprints of China's broader MOOC community. More importantly, these discourses, especially when well documented and easily accessible on open social media like Baidu Bar (as oppose to more private social media like QQ Qun), may stimulate more and critical reflections and deliberations not only within the MOOC communities but also the general public.

DISCUSSIONS

The three MOOC communities utilized different social media to promote MOOCs as well as to support their targeted MOOCers. Table 4 highlights some of the characteristics of the three selected MOOC communities.

As indicated in the following table, MOOC communities vary by member profile, activity, choice of social media, and several other factors. There are some shared characteristics among them. For instance, all MOOC communities utilize multiple media, new emerging social media, and traditional print press. They also find myriad ways to promote MOOCs within the community as well as cross-communities and to the general public.

As shown in this study, social media serve different purposes and audiences. For example, Sina Weibo is frequently used for information communication and MOOC promotion among organizations and to disseminate knowledge and information to the general public. In contrast, Baidu Bar and Web Portal are considered virtual homes of individual MOOCers, where they initiate and participate in a plethora of interesting and engaging member communications within the community. In addition, there are rich and extended collaborative knowledge constructions, experience sharing, and peer support that are documented in these social media sites. There are also many valuable and creative learning artifacts that are generated and shared among members of these communities. Evidently, members of these communities are comfortable talking to each other, asking for help, offering help, challenging other's opinions, and sharing a sense of ownership of the community.

Targeting different MOOCer groups, the MOOC communities have each implemented various strategies to accommodate and serve their members, and also to attract potential MOOCers. MA, for example, is the largest MOOC virtual community and is sponsored by promising and successful companies. Therefore, it is able to provide MOOC scholarships through partnerships. It can also organize large-scale online or face-to-face events involving world leaders in the field of MOOCs and open education, such as the Coursera founder, Harvard ChinaX teaching crew, well-liked MOOC professors from top universities in China and overseas, and many others.

ZUT.MG likewise is able to leverage university support and resources to help college students become better prepared for MOOC challenges. Regular offline seminars and university-wide events with MOOCers and MOOC instructors provide extra support and motivation for MOOC learning, and to some degree translate the MOOC experiences into blended, collaborative learning with rich social presence of both learners and instructors.

Table 4
Characteristics of the Three MOOC Communities

Characteristic	MOOC Academy (MA)	ZUT MOOC Group (ZUT.MG)	High School MOOCer Bar (HS.MB)
Founder	GuoKr.com	ZUT students taken MOOCs	High School (and younger) MOOCers
Member Profile	Diverse: • MOOCers • MOOC instructors • MOOC institutions • MOOC advocates (e.g., organizations, institutions, individuals, and companies) • MOOC groups or organizations	Current college or university students, mostly at ZUT	High school students or younger, including elementary school and middle school students
Activity Format	• Online • Local events • Blended	• Regular local events • Online	• Online only • No intent to organize any local/offline events due to distributed member locations
Community Activity	• Translation • Subtitle • Course announcements • Course notes • MOOCer experience sharing • MOOC scholarships • Large-scale MOOC promotion events	• Course announcements • Notes sharing • English-learning • F2F gatherings of MOOCers • Connecting famous professors with MOOCers • MOOC-related seminars and learning activities	• Strategically structured study groups • Course recommendations and suggestions • Notes sharing • Translation • Subtitle • Peer support • Various support Groups
Social Media	Sina Weibo (userID: MOOC Academy) http://www.weibo.com/ guokrmooc?from=feed &loc=nickname MA web portal: http://mooc.guokr.com WeChat	Sina Weibo (userID: ZUT MOOC Group) http://www.weibo.com/u/3772439187 Sina Blog: http://blog.sina.com.cn/s/articlelist_3772439187_0_1.html QQ Qun WeChat (official public ID: zjutmooc)	Sina Weibo (no community ID, leaders are active on Weibo via personal userIDs) Baidu Bar: http://tieba.baidu.com/ QQ Qun

HS.MB, unlike the other two, is completely online with no face-to-face events. It is strictly volunteer based, with highly dedicated peer leaders, and has shown a strong evidence of collaboration and peer support within the community. The highly structured learning groups, each with substantial support from the HS.MB community must have helped tremendously with these extremely busy and stressed high school MOOCers. Their cooperative approach to MOOC learning and serious commitment to peer support place them among the most successful virtual learning communities, as demonstrated by exemplary MOOCers in the community. Across these MOOC communities, there are remarkable contributions of their leaders and volunteers to the broader MOOC community in China (e.g., Huanzai, 2014, Zhjiang University of Technology MOOC Group, 2014).

According to the two surveys GuoKr.com conducted in 2013 and 2014 (MOOC Academy, 2013, 2014b), Chinese-speaking MOOCers are still mostly in developed cities and areas of China. In addition, 70% of MOOCers take courses on computers. However, only 11.5% of them visited MOOC sites and resources on cell phones and slightly more (i.e., 17.6%) utilized iPads for their MOOC-related activities and visitations.

Many other challenges remain. For instance, language barriers and the slow Internet speed for downloading or streaming course videos are the two most frustrating challenges for MOOCers in China. The MOOC communities, as found in the present study, have certainly helped address such challenges and issues, such as by forming voluntary service groups for translation and subtitling. They have also facilitated the sharing of MOOC resources on domestic cloud services. In addition, these communities have created unique means for organizational resource sharing such as by providing ESL seminars, archiving and sharing MOOC-related learning events online, and other face-to-face events. There are also frequent, humorous "gentle whipping" efforts to motivate MOOCers as well as the use of social media to connect MOOCers with MOOC instructors. Across their efforts, these social media communities in China have found novel and highly important ways to add to the growing, domestically hosted OER and MOOCs.

It is through these newfound connections and relationships that much success is occurring that is vital to document. MA, for instance, is proud of the relatively higher MOOC completion rate of its members, more than 10% as compared to 7% or lower as reported in earlier studies outside of China (Agarwala, 2013; Parr, 2013; Weller, 2014).

The comparative analysis of the three distinctive yet representative MOOC communities also sheds lights on how to leverage social media for community building and MOOC learning support. With the wide variety of MOOC communities (e.g., location-based, course-specific, subject-focused, organizational or institutional, demographic-specific, or otherwise), the selection of social media for the specific MOOC community is closely related to the social, cultural, and contextual needs of its members. Such a finding was not unexpected given earlier research related to social media choices and behaviors from a social constructivist perspective (e.g., Fulk, Schmitz & Steinfield, 1990; Fulk, 1993; Zhang & Ge, 2006). For example, as shown in Table 2, WeChat and QQ Qun, which are more mobile-friendly, are particularly popular among MOOCers for building location-based, subject- or course-specific communities.

Social Media for MOOC Communities: Public or Private?

It is highly interesting that many MOOC communities have chosen to build a "private" or otherwise protected virtual home on selected social media, where members may feel more comfortable to ask questions and seek timely assistance. With higher levels of privacy and security, those private or protected communities may not be able to create a community-constructed knowledge base on such more private social media apps, due to their technical characteristics. Thus, at the same time, some MOOC communities, like the High School MOOCers in this study, realized the critical benefits of an open Web portal, where anyone, members or non-members, may access and participate on the user-contributed community site. All three of the MOOC communities included in this study have strategically opted both public (e.g., Sina Weibo, Sina blog, Baidue Bar, Web portals) and somewhat private (e.g., WeChat, QQ Qun) social media to serve different purposes. Other MOOC communities may find such balanced approaches valuable and practical as well.

The three communities in this study all consistently applied multiple social media, through consistent and repetitive course announcements, MOOC instructor highlights, MOOCer highlights, and MOOCer testimonials to promote either specific MOOC or MOOCs in general among community members and beyond. In addition, a combination of online, offline, and blended events and diverse activities empowered MOOCers and their MOOC communities with great benefits (e.g., social presences, member bonding, trust building, peer support, etc.). Taking advantage of executive and administrative support, organizational MOOC communities like the one at ZUT would be able to transform the new, foreign concept of a MOOC into lively and engaging, blended learning experiences through regular local, face-to-face events. By the same token, location-based MOOC communities may schedule regular meetings or gatherings for MOOCers to network as well as learn together.

Members of the High School MOOCer Bar were definitely among the most busy and most stressed in China. Despite the notoriously heavy workload at school, these grade-school MOOCers managed to build a supportive online community, complete multiple MOOCs, help fellow MOOCers, and contribute to the broader MOOC community through volunteer services.

Exemplary leadership and rigorous peer support are the most critical factors of such a successful MOOC community. The High School MOOCer Bar has demonstrated plenty of creative and effective strategies for MOOC communities, including the thoughtful ways of forming collaborative learning groups, task allocations among group members, and various supports by volunteers in each group as well as cross groups. These strategies may be adapted to build and strengthen similar MOOC communities.

The following is a list of 15 selected strategies, as found in this study, which could contribute to the success of MOOC communities.

1. Utilize a variety of social media for different purposes;

2. Provide constant support and motivation on social media, with a touch of humor;

3. Provide a virtual space for user-contributed community portal and socializing activities (online, offline, or blended);

4. Recognize peer support efforts by collecting and reporting peer-rated helpfulness and the number of help attempts;

5. Share fellow MOOCer stories, including the success, the challenges, and the lessons learned;

6. Introduce MOOC instructors as normal people outside of their MOOC offerings;

7. Connect MOOCers with instructors, online, offline, or blended in social events or learning activities;

8. Encourage and recognize collaboration, cooperation, and volunteer work;

9. Share and add resources in cloud storages;

10. Organize regular community events (online, offline, blended, etc.);

11. Build and distribute a collective MOOC calendar for targeted MOOCers;

12. Leverage geo-/social functions of mobile devices and apps for just-in-time support or "near me" support;

13. Send or push friendly reminders of MOOC strategies, events, resources, etc. regularly and frequently on social media and/or via mobile devices;

14. Add to the growing MOOC resources and OER in native and foreign languages;

15. Communicate and interact with other MOOC communities and advocates.

CONCLUSIONS

As technology became increasingly available and affordable in China, Internet access and use proliferated. In fact, there are now over 420 million mobile Internet users, 26.5% of them were in the rural regions and areas (China Internet Network Information Center, 2013). Popular social media, such as Weibo had attracted more than 2.5 billion users by December 2011 (China Internet Network Information Center). As people in China and other Chinese speaking countries increasingly obtain access to the Internet, the numbers of Internet and social media users in rural and remote China will undoubtedly grow dramatically as well. As this occurs, MOOC communities, leveraged through various social media may become more accessible for those in need in rural and remote areas. Such MOOC communities will be vital in the education opportunities brought to Chinese citizens as well as to their ultimate level of successes and accomplishments.

As shown in this study, social media, when well utilized may offer strong support for MOOCers in their course selections, knowledge construction, and overall levels of satisfaction and confidence in future MOOC enrollments. Such social media communities may also promote MOOCs to the general public in engaging ways. Strategies and activities as demonstrated in these cases may be applicable to help MOOCers in other countries and regions, improve and sustain their level of motivation. The ideas and strategies, as found in this study, might also elevate MOOC completion rates as well as other measures of engagement and overall success.

It is important to point out that this study did not collect or analyze the rich, textual and multimedia data on some of the more private social media, including QQ Qun and WeChat communities that were password protected. Future research might seek appropriate participant consent to explore with more depth how MOOC communities function on those social media. Educational data mining (e.g., Hung & Zhang, 2008, 2012) and text mining (e.g., Ampofo, Collister, O'Loughlin, & Chadwick, in press) of the big data sets generated on those open social media sites (e.g., Sina Weibo, Baidu Bar, and Sina blog) may further push the research frontier on MOOCs and open education with more sociological analyses and deep ethnographic insights on MOOC learning communities.

References

Agarwala, M. (2013, March 7). *A research summary of MOOC completion rates*. EdLab, Teachers College, Columbia University. Retrieved from http://edlab.tc.columbia.edu/index.php?q=node/8990

Ampofo, L., Collister, S., O'Loughlin, B., & Chadwick, A. (in press). Text mining and social media: When quantitative meets qualitative, and software meets humans. In P. Halfpenny & R. Procter (Eds.) *Innovations in digital research methods*. London: Sage.

Bildner, E. (2013a). *A new partnership to bring Coursera to the hundreds of millions of Chinese learners across the world*. Coursera Official Blog. Retrieved from http://blog.coursera.org/post/63406806112/a-new-partnership-to-bring-coursera-to-the-hundreds-of

Bildner, E. (2013b). *How to earn 40 certificates: An interview with China's MOOC Superstar*. Coursera Official Blog. Retrieved from http://blog.coursera.org/post/71034696695/how-to-earn-40-certificates-an-interview-with-chinas

China Internet Network Information Center (2013). *The 30th statistical report on Internet development in China [online]*. Retrieved from http://www1.cnnic.cn/IDR/ReportDownloads/201310/P020131029430558704972.pdf

Creswell, J. W. (2003). *Research design: Qualitative, quantitative, and mixed method approaches*. Thousand Oaks, CA: Sage Publications.

Creswell, J. W. (2005). *Educational research: Planning, conducting, and evaluating quantitative and qualitative research*. New Jersey: Prentice Hall.

Creswell, J. W., & Clark, V.L.P. (2007). *Designing and conducting mixed methods research*. Thousand Oaks, CA: Sage Publications.

Ebner, M., Lienhardt, C., Rohs, M., & Meyer, I. (2010). Microblogs in higher education – A chance to facilitate informal and process-oriented learning? *Computers and Education, 55*(1), 92-100.

Ebner, M., & Maurer, H. (2009). Can weblogs and microblogs change traditional scientific writing? *Future Internet, 1*(1), 47-58.

Fulk, J. (1993). Social construction of communication technology. *Academy of Management Journal, 36*(5), 921-950.

Fulk, J., Schmitz, J., & Steinfield, C. W. (1990). A social influence model of technology use. In J. Fulk & C. Steinfield (Eds.), *Organizations and communications technology* (pp. 117- 140). Newbury Park, CA: Sage.

Huanzai (2014). *Story 4: Millenniums meet MOOC: A knowledge hunter*, GuoKr.com. Retrieved online from GuoKr official website at: http://www.guokr.com/post/622876/

Hung, J., & Zhang, K. (2008). Analyzing online learning behaviors and activity patterns and making predictions with data mining techniques in online teaching, *Journal of Online Learning and Teaching, 4*(4), 426-437.

Hung, J., & Zhang, K. (2012). Examining mobile learning trends 2003-2008: A categorical meta-trend analysis using text mining techniques, *Journal of Computing in Higher Education, 24*(1).

Junco, R., Heiberger, G., & Loken, E. (2011). The effect of Twitter on college student engagement and grades. *Journal of Computer Assisted Learning, 27*(2), 119-132. doi: 10.1111/j.1365-2729.2010.00387.x

MOOC Academy. (2013, November 21). *China's MOOC learners profiles*, retrieved August 11, 2014 from MOOC Academy Official Website at: http://mooc.guokr.com/opinion/437530/

MOOC Academy. (2014a, May 19). *An Introduction to the MOOC Academy Website*. Retrieved from MOOC Academy Official Website at http://mooc.guokr.com/post/605193/

MOOC Academy. (2014b, August 11). *The report on 2014 MOOC learners survey*. Retrieved from MOOC Academy Official Website at http://mooc.guokr.com/opinion/437642/

Pappano, L. (2012, November 2). The year of the MOOC. *The New York Times*. Retrieved from the World Wide Web at: http://edinaschools.org/cms/lib07/MN01909547/Centricity/Domain/272/The%20Year%20of%20the%20MOOC%20NY%20Times.pdf

Parr, C. (2013, May 9). Mooc completion rates 'below 7%. *Times Higher Education*. Retrieved from http://www.timeshighereducation.co.uk/news/mooc-completion-rates-below-7/2003710.article

Patton, M. Q. (1990). *Qualitative evaluation and research methods* (2nd ed.). Newbury Park, CA: Sage Publications, Inc.

Santos, F. M., & Eisenhardt, K. M. (2004). Multiple case study. In M. S. Lewis-Beck, A. Bryman & T. F. Liao (Eds.), *Encyclopedia of social science research methods* (1st Ed.). Thousand Oaks, CA: SAGE Publications, Inc.

Shen, Y. (2011). *Updates on ROST Weibo Search Tools*. Retrieved from http://blog.sciencenet.cn/home.php?mod=space&uid=239936&do=blog&id=414891

Wang, X., Yao, Y., & Ji. S. (2012, November 21). "Rumor Breaker," GuoKr is 2 years old. *Xinhua Daily Telegraph*. Retrieved from http://news.xinhuanet.com/mrdx/2012-11/21/c_131988558.htm

Weller, M. (2014). *MOOC research initiative final report: Characteristics and completion rates of distributed and centralised MOOCs*. Retrieved from http://www.moocresearch.com/wp-content/uploads/2014/06/C9131_WELLER_MOOC-Research-Initiative-OU.pdf

Yin, R. K. (2009). *Case study research: Design and methods* (4th ed.). Thousand Oaks, CA: Sage Publications, Inc.

Zhang, K. (2011). Courseware intellectual property, open courseware and online education. In R. Ouyang & X. C. Wang (Eds.), *Handbook of educational technology*, 231-249. Beijing, China: People's University Press.

Zhang, K., & Gao, F. (2014). Social media for informal science learning in China: A case study. *Knowledge Management & E-Learning: An International Journal, 6*(3), 262–280.

Zhang, K., & Ge, X. (2006). The dynamics of online collaborative learning: Team task, group development, peer relationship, and communication media. In A. D. de Figueiredo & A. A. Alfonso (Eds.), *Managing learning in virtual settings: The role of context*. 98-116. Hershey, PA: Idea Group.

Zhang, K., Liang, L., & Sang, X. (2013). Educational technology in China: Past & Present. In X. Li (Ed.). *Education in China: Cultural influences, global perspectives and social challenges*, 271-288. Hauppauge, NY: Nova Science Publishers.

Zhang, K., Peng, S. W. & Hung, J. (2009). Online collaborative learning in a project-based learning environment in Taiwan: A Case study on undergraduate students' perspectives. *Educational Media International, 46*(2), 123-135.

Zhejiang University of Technology MOOC Group (2014, March 2). *A brief introduction on ZUT MOOC Group*. Zhejiang University of Technology MOOC Group official blog. Retrieved from http://blog.sina.com.cn/s/blog_e0dada930101p8io.html

Zhou, T. (2010, September 28). *Baidu TieBa traffic is over 10,00,000,000*. Finance News on iFeng.com. Retrieved from http://finance.ifeng.com/roll/20100928/2660578.shtml

Ke Zhang is Associate Professor at Wayne State University in the USA. Her research focuses on e-learning, mobile learning technologies and social media, and big data research and applications in educational technology research and development. Her research publications are translated into and/or cited in languages such as Armenian, Chinese, French, Italian, Spanish, Portuguese and more. Her work is adapted to guide research and practices of e-learning and mobile learning in different countries and various settings. Her collaborative research is funded by NIH with multi-million grants. She serves on the editorial boards for highly regarded scholarly journals, and plays active leadership roles in international professional organizations. She has delivered keynote presentations and invited talks in Chile, China, Hong Kong, Japan, Malaysia, the UAE, and the USA. Dr. Zhang has consulted for international organizations like the World Bank, national government and agencies, corporations and educational institutions, both in USA and overseas. Inquiries are welcome by email to ke.zhang@wayne.edu.

International Jl. on E-Learning (2015) **14**(3) Special Issue, 331-350

The Emergent Role of the MOOC Instructor: A Qualitative Study of Trends Toward Improving Future Practice

SARAH HAAVIND
Pepperdine University, USA
Sarah.Haavind@pepperdine.edu

CYNTHIA SISTEK-CHANDLER
National University, USA
cchandler@nu.edu

Massive Open Online Courses (MOOCs) differ from other teaching environments in both the potentially "massive" number of participants and the "open" aspect of teaching in a public forum. Early MOOC instructors have of necessity worn many hats: subject matter expert, facilitator, researcher, producer, director, and curator. These evolving and interwoven responsibilities, and questions about how the role of MOOC instructor is currently being performed, were the catalysts for this investigation. Eight MOOC instructors were interviewed for this study. Each shared perceptions of the instructional assets required for success in a MOOC. Using a case study approach and qualitative interview methodology, this study chronicles current practice with an eye toward emergent, effective practice. Whether a collaborative, connectivist cMOOC style or video-lecture-based xMOOC style, or something in between, the role of the instructor is largely pedagogical—oriented toward planning and preparing the MOOC experience. As a result, real-time, engagement from MOOC instructors during a course likely has little effect on most participants.

INTRODUCTION

Many different instructor roles have been on display in the early days of Massive Open Online Courses or "MOOCs," including producer, director, facilitator, subject matter expert, curator, and researcher. What separates MOOCs from other learning environments—and particularly from other online learning venues—are first, the potentially "massive" number of participants, and, second, the "open" aspect of teaching in a public forum. The question arises, Do MOOC instructors also play the role of star by attracting a "celebrity" following? This and other questions led to the present examination of the roles early MOOC instructors are adopting, and how role selection is defined during this emergent stage.

The article begins by comparing MOOC-style content delivery with more typical types of online instruction. We then chronicle our exploration of the roles MOOC instructors are playing, with consideration of recently published articles and reports. Guiding this research were interviews with eight instructors who shared their experiences and insights during May and June 2014. We conclude with the understanding that even though it appears that there are two contrasting types of MOOC pedagogies—the collaborative, community-oriented "cMOOC" and the more content-broadcast, lecture-oriented "xMOOC"—the instructor role is minimized in both. Instead, automated grading, peer participation, and the incorporation of numerous teaching assistants are often the most salient elements during the time frame that a MOOC is live. Instructors are either absent or simply part of the crowd; in effect, they are no more or less noticeable and relevant than anyone else who attends the MOOC.

ONLINE LEARNING

Instructor roles in more traditional online courses set the foundation for instruction in the MOOC environment. Berge (1995), for example, recognized early in the development of online pedagogy that the complexity of the instructional role involved two types of interaction: (1) interaction with content, and (2) interpersonal interactions among peers as well as interpersonal interaction with the instructor. In addition to analyzing these two types of interaction, Berge also discussed four instructional roles: pedagogical, technological, social, and managerial (Liu, Bonk, Magjuka, Lee, & Su, 2005). Of course, these instructional roles are essential in many learning environments, not just in online learning. However, an online course instructor must also coordinate, curate, construct, and create the experience between instructor and student, student and student, student and text, and student to community. And she must do this behind a computer screen.

Over the past two decades of Internet-based learning, new practices in achieving interactivity in online education have emerged. Examples of such techniques for interactivity include assigning greater importance to discussions in text-based forums and designing prompts for discussion that foster extended peer dialogue (Collison, Elbaum, Haavind, & Tinker, 2000; Haavind, 2007). Effective practices also include increasing facilitation practices, such as weaving threads (Collison et al., 2000; Harasim 1993; Rohfeld & Hiemstra, 1995), and creating relevant and engaging learning challenges that take advantage of online tools and geographically distributed learners (Bonk & Zhang, 2008).

Pedagogical concepts such as social knowledge construction (Scardamalia & Bereiter, 1994) and connectivism (Downes, 2005; Siemens, 2005) have advanced this progress by integrating technological practices for deepening learning. Most potentially disruptive, or perhaps revolutionary, in terms of how classroom teaching and learning are traditionally defined, is how knowledge learning is moving away from subject matter experts and shifting toward the creation of knowledge among students. This shift in learning control, in fact, changes the online teaching dynamic from one in which the ownership of knowledge rests with the subject matter expert to one in which all participants share, negotiate, and build upon such ownership. This progression in pedagogy from lecture-based teaching toward more distributed teaching and distributed learning is enabled by new Web technologies.

MOOC instruction sprang from the potential of new technologies to deliver instruction to a massive audience. For example, a private company has developed for the Open University in the UK proprietary Web technologies specifically intended for teaching in a MOOC environment. That private company—a Web technology creator called FutureLearn— is wholly owned by the UK Open University whose partners include over 20 UK and international universities and institutions such as the British Council, the British Library, and the British Museum. So not only is the platform unique, but the archived cultural and educational content are being curated to be delivered exclusively in an online format. As this process occurs, culture and knowledge are being shared with the masses.

MOOCs may be perceived as the next natural extension of distance learning; they began first as paper assignments posted via mail service, were later delivered via radio and television programming, and eventually exploded through cable television. More recently, we have witnessed the rise of online technologies for delivering educational opportunities, culminating, for now, with massively open access via MOOCs. However, as with each previous iteration in the expansion of the geographical reach of education and training beyond the immediate four walls of a single classroom, teaching practices that optimize learning must be reexamined and reevaluated for effectiveness. Are MOOCS just very large, open courses delivered over the Internet, or does that massiveness and openness require adjustments and revisions to teaching practices that optimize learning opportunities for the participants at scale? This article examines the growing body of research that documents early MOOCs. It then considers specific experiences of eight MOOC instructors (I-1 through I-8) to pinpoint where we stand in this emergent field with regard to teaching effectively at scale.

EXPLORING THE ROLE OF THE INSTRUCTOR IN A MOOC

Early MOOCs

In 2008, Canadian academic David Cormier coined the term "MOOC." He used it to characterize a new type of online course that was designed by George Siemens and Stephen Downes in their course, "Connectivism and Connected Knowledge." Other early MOOCs have been mentioned in the literature; Davidson (2013), for example, indicates MOOC-like courses were first offered in 2006 and 2007 by the Humanities, Arts, Science, Technology Alliance and Collaboratory (HASTAC).

According to Siemens, the purpose of the MOOC course was:

> ...for people to experience what it means to be a part of a social, technical system of learning where the teacher's voice is not an essential hub but, instead, a node in an overall network." (Cited in Hollands & Tirthali, 2014, p. 32).

Since the early MOOCs, many more have been designed and offered to millions of participants worldwide. Along the way, the role of instructors has varied significantly.

We came to this research with questions and concerns about how the role of the instructor is constrained, expanded, or otherwise altered by the "massive" characteristic of MOOCs and the "massive, open, online" nature of facilitating courses of this magnitude. As seasoned online instructors of 14 plus years each, and having spent our careers in education moving gradually away from teacher-centered practices to more student-centered approaches, the thought of a different structure of facilitation was perplexing. How can an instructor relinquish the facilitation role and also rely on automatic grading or grading by someone else? How can personalization and individual attention be given to a massive number of students? Dividing students into large numbers of study groups seems both unwieldy and unpromising. Can automated grading or machine feedback, combined with the use of peer feedback and study groups, be sufficient for students' needs? Should teaching assistants and experts be called upon to extend such interactivity and feedback?

At the same time, some participants might be pleased with their new-found open access to savvy lecturers or experts in fast-growing fields. Other students might be delighted at the opportunity to enroll in courses designed by the "rock stars" of education. While this latter option appears to present an unarguable advantage, future research and querying of enrollees will be needed to test the strength of the "rock star" motivation hypothesis for learner course enrollment.

Variations and Classifications of MOOCs

Since the first Connectivist, or cMOOC in 2006, a variety of classifications have emerged to describe MOOCs. These classifications may focus on pedagogical interactions and outcomes or on the participant's experience. In our examination of the literature, we found several MOOC classification frameworks (Clark, 2013; Conole, 2013; Ross, et al. 2004) that, in our interviews, fit the instructors/interviewees to varying degrees. The field is rapidly developing and the research is rapidly evolving. Thus, the following information about MOOCs and MOOC research summarizes the lenses available to us at the time of our writing.

Ross, Sinclair, Knox, Bayne, and Macleod (2014) identify three instructor types in MOOCs, whereas Reeves and Hedberg (2014) further categorize "cMOOCs" and "xMOOCs" and add "pMOOCs." The notion of the pMOOC recognizes that there are blended models in between the other two. Swan, Day, Bogle, and van Pooyen (2014) identify teaching-learning tasks and frame MOOCs based on specific criteria. All of these ideas related to MOOCs are further described below.

It is important to note that each MOOC type serves a different purpose including delivery of content (xMOOCs), opportunities to connect participants (cMOOCs), and the creation of authentic projects or products (pMOOCs). xMOOCs for example are typically highly structured course experiences. In fact, Ross et al. (2014) refer to xMOOCs as prescribed pathways that are "institutionally rooted" (p. 58). As such, the role of the instructor in cMOOCs vs. xMOOCs is vastly different, reflecting the expected differences encountered in face-to-face courses that are either collaborative or competency-based. Ross et al. (2014) describe three forms of teacher roles in a MOOC environment: "the distant 'rock star' lecturer, the co-participant or facilitator within a network, and the automated processes that serve as proxy tutor and assessor" (p. 58). According to the authors, these "teacher typologies play out in the literature in two basic forms of MOOC—the connectivist or 'cMOOC,' and the institutionally rooted, highly structured 'xMOOC'" (p. 58).

The instructor role in cMOOCs, which emerged primarily from Canadian instructors such as Siemens, Cormier, and Downes, is highly interactive. As a result, even if contact per student or "direct touch" of the instructor to student is low, the role is active in establishing connections. In contrast, Ross et al. refer to the emergence of the instructor as a "celebrity teacher." In commenting on this celebrity status, Rodriguez argues that the xMOOC professor is taking on the role of "actor-producer" (Rodriguez, 2012, p.7). In xMOOCs such as those coming out of edX (Harvard, MIT, and Stanford) or Coursera and Udacity (both venture capital-supported, independent start-ups), students learn material primarily from recorded video lectures and resources. They must pass auto-graded tests to show proficiency in order to earn certificates of completion or subject their work to peer assessment guided by rubrics. In fact, according to University of Georgia Emeritus Professor Tom Reeves (personal correspondence) "several of the xMOOCs I have personally completed relied on peer assessment rather than on automated scoring." Not surprisingly, an xMOOC is described as being able to operate with "minimal involvement" from the instructor (Ross et al., p.59).

The Role of Pedagogy

Swan et al. (2014) suggest a tool for characterizing the pedagogical approaches applied in a MOOC and have categorized the role of the MOOC teacher on a scale of one to five, where "one" is typified as teacher-centered and "five" represents a student-centered instructional approach (pp. 75-76). Swan et al. offer four criteria for teacher-centeredness: one size fits all, deadlines are set and firm, automated grading takes place with little or no human response, and the dominant form of communication is one-way from the instructor. In contrast, indicators of student-centeredness include choice in ways of indicating acquisition of knowledge, self-pacing, generative assessments, and active discussion boards that are responded to and/or or graded by the instructor.

As previously mentioned, a third type of MOOC, the Project MOOC or pMOOC, is generally a combination of the xMOOC and the cMOOC. Here the focus is to design a project that is reviewed by peers using a rubric or by external experts serving as "clients" of the learners. Course completion requirements in a pMOOC typically include reviewing a number of projects designed by peers.

A fourth type of MOOC features a hybrid (hMOOC) approach where part of the learning occurs massively and openly online and part occurs in a face-to-face (FTF) setting. Many of the Open University courses began by using the FTF setting with classes of 1,000 or more and then migrated to the online xMOOC or cMOOC.

A fifth type, the mini-MOOC or mMOOC category, emerged when we interviewed Instructor 8 (I-8). Like other MOOC types, mMOOCs offer open access but with less emphasis on massive participation—generally fewer than 500 enrollees. Hollands and Tirthali (2014) define mMOOC courses as "educational experiences delivered online to large numbers of participants, akin to a webinar" (p. 48).

The second instructor we interviewed (I-2) indicated that his MOOC fit several categories of the xMOOC and yet was partly a cMOOC since I-2 was responsive in the moment and became an active player in and during his MOOC. Instructors (and assistants) made active changes "on the fly" deviating from the original plan. This category is still emerging and could be considered as a sixth category or adaptive MOOC (aMOOC)—an environment that changes based on the dynamics of the masses.

As previously mentioned, other classifications, taxonomies, and categories continue to appear in the literature. One interesting category coined by Sylvia Moessinger (2013) in her MOOCs Around the World blog series is a "MOOClative"— a category she refers to as a MOOC, but that is actually a derivative of a MOOC. Moessinger classifies this genre of MOOC "as online educational resources that have a lot in common with MOOCs but do not quite fit the MOOC framework because they are either not massive, not entirely free, not really a complete course or do not easily fit in any of the above classifications" (Moessinger Blog, 2013).

METHODOLOGY

Interviews

This qualitative research began by conducting informational interviews with MOOC instructors we knew or who were referred to us by colleagues in the field. We also sought to include interviewees from several countries, from a variety of subject areas, some who taught contemporary topics such as gamification, and others who taught more traditional subjects such as creative writing. Although the net was cast wide to potentially include over 25 MOOC instructors, we concluded the study with eight (seven males and one female). We attempted to reach MOOC instructors from other institutions (EdX and Harvard) but did not have responses within the timeframe for this study.

An interview protocol (Table 1) guided our discussion with each instructor to gather perceptions of instructional assets that an effective MOOC instructor must possess to make a MOOC successful. Eight questions were carefully formulated to obtain perceptions about the instructional role while also gathering demographic information about the instructor. All interviews were conducted either by Skype, by phone, or by email. The voice and web interviews were over one hour in duration and in some cases were followed up with clarifying questions. The interviewees selected their preferred method for the interviews.

Table 1
Interview Protocol

1. What compelled you to teach a MOOC?
2. When and where was it offered, how many students enrolled, what was the name of the MOOC class, and what was the timeframe?
3. How long have you been teaching online?
4. What characteristics do you feel made you an effective MOOC instructor?
5. What activities were included in your role as instructor?
6. How would you characterize the interactions you had with the students in your MOOC?
7. How many hours were you/other instructors spending online each week?
8. If you have an opportunity to teach a MOOC again, what might you do differently?

We reviewed the articles and reports that form a growing body of literature on the topic and compared what we learned with the experiences our eight instructors reported from their perspectives. By using a case study approach (Merriam, 1998; Stake, 1978/2000) and qualitative interview methodology, this study chronicles current practice with an eye toward emergent, best practice concerning MOOCs and their still-evolving derivatives.

MOOC Types

Table 2 illustrates the landscape of five MOOC types. It is organized by the most common typology in the emerging literature and shows where each of the eight MOOC instructors we interviewed best fits. Instructor and course details are anonymous to preserve confidentiality. Our eight interviewees spanned three countries (Canada, the United States, and the United Kingdom) and their MOOC students participated from all over the globe.

Table 2
MOOC Interviewees and MOOC Type Classification

Instructor #	cMOOC	xMOOC	hMOOC	pMOOC	mMOOC	# of participants & percentage of completers
I-1			X			4000 1% (40)
I-2	X	X				300 15% (45)
I-3	X					20,000+ 15%
I-4	X					360+ not assessed
I-5				X		20,000 5% (1,000)
I-6		X				220,000 total over three sessions 9% (20,000)
I-7		X				30,000 2% (700)
I-8					X	500 26% (115)

ANALYZING THE INSTRUCTOR ROLE

The second part of this study considers insights from the literature related to specific roles MOOC instructors have assumed to date, combined and extended by the experiences and perceptions of the eight instructors interviewed. Overall, we discovered that the instructors we spoke with generally fit into the typology of cMOOC and xMOOC, with a few resembling the pMOOC and mMOOC variations. A number of issues and trends related to the instructor role surfaced in our interviews, with topics ranging from forms of feedback and responsiveness, to open access and security, to meeting the needs of a global audience. We begin with a brief review of how the role is initially being characterized and where that path might lead.

In discussing cMOOCs, or student-centered "Connectivist" MOOCs, Cormier and Siemens (2010) suggest several vital roles that apply to educators in all online courses, not just the massive, open ones. Among these emerging instructor roles are amplifying important course ideas and concepts; curating readings and resources; "wayfinding" or assisting learners to rely on social sense-making through networks; aggregating or displaying patterns in discussions or content; content finding and filtering; supporting learners' critical thinking; modeling or displaying successful information and interaction patterns; and finally, staying present by maintaining continual instructor presence during the course.

Connectivist MOOCs value these complex roles as they are grounded in the roles and practices of an online instructor. Interestingly, one cMOOC facilitator we interviewed explained that responding to conversations in the online discussions felt more like "working on a nest in a forest," as opposed to the more common online facilitation role of advancing conversation for the class (I-4 personal correspondence, May 2014). There is a clear shift in the scope of potential instructor impact in learning in a cMOOC. In such environments, instruction tends to feel more similar to authoring a book or curating a museum exhibit and then having relatively little control over what participants take from the experience.

Another cMOOC instructor (I-3) refers to himself as a "Captain of a Ship." The ship in this case carried 20,000 passengers. I-3 has been teaching in a massive environment for a decade. Prior to teaching his first cMOOC, his traditional course was taken by approximately 3,000 students per year, over a period of eight years, with FTF contact and digital assignments. The success of the MOOC course, he feels, is dependent upon the ongoing and continuous improvement of materials, strong content, and the inclusion of guest lecturers from the field (I-3, personal correspondence, May 2014).

As did a number of the eight instructors we interviewed, Instructor 3 wrote all the course content himself. With such large interest and enrollment, he has the data to support his claim of success of the 20,000+ student MOOC. It was delivered by an institutionally owned platform and facilitated by four teachers, giving each teacher/facilitator 5,000 students. How could quality instruction and assessment of so many assignments take place in such massive enrollment? The nature of the subject, writing fiction, allowed for peer review of writing; the Web platform randomly and anonymously assigned work among the four teachers and among peers who reviewed work as an iterative process. Instructor 3 refers to the massive navigation of content by so many students as "crowd surfing" at a rock concert: students "surfed" over discussions, trying to "hook-up" with like-minded participants. Student participation during that five-week period is impressive—over 100,000 postings per week (in addition to the weekly assignments or papers reviewed).

According to Ross et al., cMOOC instructors in the extreme tend to instruct less, choosing instead to facilitate and guide students through self-directed learning. For the xMOOC instructor, once the video lectures have been recorded, the requirements established, and the auto-grading system set in place, what role remains? Although this question may be rhetorical, the MOOC concept pushes those in higher education, faculty members in particular, for direction. Teaching and constructing a MOOC may simply be another form of scholarship, comparable to writing a book or curating content.

Emerging Issues and Trends

Our discussions with instructors highlighted a few emerging issues and trends relevant to the role of instructor. Such trends and issues include the feasibility of providing feedback to students, concerns about the personal safety of instructors (aka "rock stars") when teaching a MOOC, and comparisons with more traditional instructor roles.

Feedback. Whether the MOOC instructor role is perceived as that of ship commander, leader, or director, what a MOOC instructor is not is a grader or provider of feedback that is deeply meaningful or personalized. In the various reports on MOOCs as well as in the comments of those we interviewed, the feedback role is typically automated, performed by peers, or conducted peripherally or almost exclusively by Teaching Assistants (TAs). Of course, responses to personal emails are also similarly impossible for one person to manage. During one MOOC course, Instructor 6 put an automatic reply on his email to address the influx of "40 emails per hour/24 hours a day during the first week of the course."

All of our interviewees reported a lack of control over the unyielding amount of student input, and a need for channeling the massiveness of student interaction through assignments, posts, discussion boards, or forums. One instructor reflected the feelings of most when he said, "Facilitators cannot give thorough analysis to every piece of work. As an experienced traditional teacher, I felt slightly negligent about not being able to [personally] check up on the work" (I-3, personal correspondence, May 2014). Another common theme is reflected in this comment: "For the first session especially, I participated actively in the discussion forums, but that only meant interacting with a very small percentage of students. I didn't advertise my email address, but several dozen students each session find it, so I often respond to questions from individuals that way. But overall, the vast majority of the communication was outbound from me rather than interactive" (I-6, personal communication, May 2014).

Open Access and Security. Two of our interviewees identified specific challenges that can ensue from offering a public course where anyone has free access with open enrollment. If there is an activity, product, platform, or content that is disliked, or even a particular professor who is not received well by some attendees, reputations become vulnerable. One such incident—where a course at Georgia Tech crashed in the first week of its 41,000 student enrollment—generated negative tweets and anger from a large number of constituents. An early course failure of this magnitude was also reported in The Chronicle of Higher Education survey (Kolowich, 2013).

> With tens of thousands of people taking each MOOC, if a small percentage of people have a negative experience for whatever reason, the discussion boards explode with complaints. Anything involving grades leads to this. Small problems (with grading, with videos, or anything else) cause tons of work in terms of damage control. (Paul Gries, University of Toronto, 2013)

Safety is an issue for students as well. Noting that student safety may be compromised by the open and massive aspects of MOOCs, Bali (2014) suggests publishing netiquette standards. However, in an open environment where someone who is locked out for misbehavior can simply re-enroll under new identifiers, it is difficult to control access. As with instructors, the reputations of students can be compromised. How can safety be ensured for either group? If students strive to protect themselves by not using their real names to enroll in a course, how can they ever use a certificate of achievement earned from the course as a credential? One of our interviewees reported being stalked by a student who lived in the same city where his university was located and who easily found his office. Unlike rock stars in the entertainment world, university academics are unlikely to be able to afford security details

Similarities and Differences in the Role of Instructor. In the early days of online learning, the related research primarily focused on whether eliciting the same level of student achievement and outcomes required instructors to have a different skill set than that typically used for FTF teaching (lecturing). Early research confirmed that for online learning to be successful, interaction is needed similar to the group dynamic that occurs in FTF teaching (Hiltz & Goldman, 2005). The debate over the differences between online and FTF teaching continues today. Instructional design for online learning has its challenges in how to effectively "chunk" material or lectures. Alternatively, as MOOCs have emerged, the focus is less on student outcomes and achievement and more on the delivery of expert content. The role and responsibility of instructors or institutions for engaging learners in MOOCs continues to be both questioned and challenged. The authors of the report MOOCs: Expectations and Reality (Hollands & Tirthali, 2014) voiced a strong statement on this topic:

It appears that few MOOC offerers [that entity or institution that offers the MOOC] are willing to address the apparently straightforward question of whether MOOC participants gain skills and knowledge as a result of their engagement in the courses. Part of this reluctance may stem from the fact that MOOCs are being pursued at many institutions for reasons other than improvement of teaching and learning. (p. 19)

The primary reasons for institutions' investing in and offering MOOCs, according to their study, include expanding reach, and building and maintaining brand (Hollands & Tirthali, 2014, p. 8).

Even if MOOCs per se turn out to be a brief trend ("like bellbottoms" suggested Siemens during his keynote at E-Learn 2013), reflections and debates about the role of teaching in a networked or connected world are not going to fade away any time soon. It is perhaps not surprising to find that the pioneering MOOC instructors have largely ignored decades of rigorous research on effective online teaching practices, particularly as it relates to individualized and personalized contact with students. In a nutshell, dozens of research studies have found student-instructor and instructor-student interactivity to be critical components of satisfaction and persistence for online learners (Anderson, 2003; Croxton, 2014). Meanwhile, the interactivity between the MOOC instructor and the student, perhaps due to the massive numbers of students, is still at a minimum. As Siemens explained, the university and the traditional courses that the instructor crafts and delivers have been designed for periodic learning, yet we are inexorably shifting to a model of continuous, lifelong learning. Hence, the effective instructional practices that are emerging through the role of the MOOC instructor will have lasting value whether the trend of free, open massive courses endures or not (Siemens, 2013).

BEST PRACTICES IN MOOCS

Best practices in MOOCs are likely those that resonate with effective practice on the non-massive scale as well. As more attention to effective practice in online teaching is gradually embraced by MOOC designers and instructors, automation can play a larger role than just grading simple response quizzes and tests. For example, highly interactive small groups and feedback-rich experiences are among the more recognized "best" practices online.

At first glance, such interaction might seem an unlikely candidate for automation, but there is increasing interest in how interactivity between and among group members can potentially be better fostered at scale using datamining technologies. For instance, a study by MIT Sloan (Kirin, Boucher

Fergusson, & Kirk Prentice, 2013) included an algorithm by Paul Goldman that is applied in Linked In and uses data analytics to connect individuals by affinity and other known associations. Other technologies emerging in Google products and elsewhere hold promise for improving feedback loops and productive interaction at scale. In fact, a study conducted by Wilkowski, Russell, and Deutsch (2014) examined the effectiveness of self-evaluation by advanced power searching and mapping with Google MOOCs. We are only in the initial stages of exploring how the mining of "big" data can positively influence online teaching and learning.

Effective Practices and Lessons Learned

Meanwhile, the analysis of eight interview transcripts as well as an analysis of the literature (Alario-Hoyos, Pérez-Sanagustín, Delgado-Kloos, Muñoz-Organero, Rodríguez-de-las-Heras, 2013; Bali, 2014; Clark, 2013; Tomkin & Charlevoix, 2014; Zhang, 2013) brought to the surface several potentially more effective instructional practices in a MOOC environment. These practices include presentation skills (think "actor" or "rock star"), strong content, managerial skills (e.g., "director" or "captain"), personalization, feedback and fostering student-centered interaction. Each is briefly discussed below.

Presentation Skills. Video presentations, albeit recorded, must be engaging and represent good inflection, diction, and articulation. It is essential to include a warm and inviting tone and to have a personable video presence. All of these qualities seem vital in a MOOC. Humor and personality, both on camera and in live classroom performances, can inspire participation. A number of our interviewees mentioned writing and then editing their scripts for video lectures. In addition to superior presentation skills, interviewees suggested that a stellar cast of actors is important, including subject matter experts and guests with engaging personalities.

Strong Content. Clearly, strong content on a relevant, timely topic helps to ensure a massive audience. One dilemma that emerged in the literature and in our discussions is the challenge of using open education resources (OERs). Typically, rigorous university courses assign scholarly reading material that may or may not be freely available or online. However, to keep access open and to accommodate a global audience, incorporating OERs is essential. The trade-off with open access can be with quality and consistency of the content.

Managerial Skills. Managerial skills are critical, including the management of TAs, course content, and flow. One interviewee mentioned assigning TAs online hours with the goal of maintaining a 24/7 global presence (I-1, personal communication, May 2014).

Personalization. Typical strategies for personalizing MOOCs are to foster small group gatherings (by geographic region, common interests, etc.), design opportunities for peer discussion and feedback, and offer multiple points of entry (including Twitter, etc.). Regular email notifications of new sessions, trending conversations, synchronous sessions, etc., help encourage continued momentum and engagement. A variety of MOOC instructors have experimented with open office hours; however, time zone differences, work responsibilities, and other variables can affect interest and attendance.

Feedback. As automatic data processing tools become increasingly sophisticated, additional instant feedback loops can be integrated. For now, auto-grading, auto-emailing, and reminders can serve some purposes, as can polling and peer discussion tools—such as email notifications of replies to threads in which a participant posts. Notice that most, if not all, of these elements do not require the instructor's active presence.

Student-Centered Interaction. Instructor 4 commented about the MOOC she co-taught that "I almost feel that the effort to be open and inclusive can have the opposite effect. Those with the big voices get the attention" (I-4, personal correspondence, May 2014). In terms of direct interactions with students, if you have thousands of them, from the instructor perspective it can be quite rewarding to be able to pick up an interesting conversation as you "surf" discussions. Instructors 1, 3, and 5 all mentioned many connections they made or deepened due to teaching a MOOC. Instructor 3 remarked that building a professional community in a growing field was his main reason for agreeing to teach his MOOC. Instructor 5 was delighted with the people he connected with while teaching his MOOC. However, while those shining star students rose to the top and drove the spotlight for a select few, the MOOC course had little impact for most.

Instructor 4 also noted the most common interactivity in the MOOC was 1:1 conversation, whether with one of the facilitators or among students. "It was impossible to keep up with the conversations ... most of my interactions with students felt more like I was investing in my own interests and curiosities about the subject matter" (I-4, personal correspondence, May 2014).

Research conducted by Hew and Cheung (2014) reports similar findings that support key challenges of teaching MOOCs: "1) difficulty in evaluating students' work, 2) having a sense of speaking into a vacuum due to the absence of student immediate feedback, 3) being burdened by the heavy demands of time and money, and 4) encountering a lack of student participation in online forums" (p. 45).

Peer-to-peer interactions are gaining focus to help solve the challenge of providing feedback to massive numbers of participants. However, to date the outcomes are unpredictable, uncontrollable, and wide-ranging. More than a rubric or instructional scaffold is needed to ensure quality feedback from a randomly assigned peer. Much like in the traditional classroom, challenges remain with peer review before a satisfying experience can be delivered for most if not all who participate. It remains to be seen how far sophisticated analytics and data mining will bring learners beyond the current state of automated grading features. In addition, though not a central focus of this study, it should at least be mentioned that providing seamless language translation in order to allow truly global conversations seems possible but is not yet reality.

In Retrospect: After the MOOC

When we asked our interviewees about what they would have liked to do but were unable to do, the feedback indicates that they felt stymied by the massive and open nature of MOOCs. For example, Instructor 6 wished to provide multiple pathways through content, calibrated peer assessment, real-world final projects, small-group collaboration among students, and the ability to review course analytics to improve materials and assessments. Instructor 4 reported that she wished to apply some of the facilitation strategies that are only feasible with smaller numbers, feeling a propensity to interact and comment on all blogs and participate in all conversations. Ironically, Instructor 6 reflected on his own instructional role, observing:

> By all indications, I am a significantly better MOOC instructor than an in-person teacher. And I've done one MOOC vs. trying hard for ten years to learn how to teach in the classroom... but it suggests the MOOC format matches better with my skills.

He then added, "I think the bar is lower for being an effective MOOC instructor today" (I-6, personal communication, May 2014).

This low bar of instruction in open, massive courses resonates in the field (Hollands & Tirthali, 2014). Given that high-quality teaching and certifiable learning are not typically essential goals for those offering MOOCs, it is not surprising that whatever role the instructor might play, it is not all that critical. Instead, other factors are perceived to be the measures of "success" for a MOOC, including quality of content, building engagement through time management (Nawrot, & Doucet, 2014), digitation of knowledge procedures (Perotta, 2014), and the ability to offer learning in an open, accessible, format.

CONCLUSIONS

The instructor role in an xMOOC clearly differs from that of a more traditional online course instructor. The MOOC instructional role shifts more to content delivery and broadcasting. Production of a MOOC is highly scripted, directed, and orchestrated. Additionally, data analytics and autograding maximize efficiency. In such a MOOC, the instructor is less of a "teacher" and more a designer and producer of content.

Overall, the purpose of MOOCs to date appears to be primarily for marketing to massive audiences. All eight interviewees are respected, highly interpersonal, passionate educators whose guidance of the student learning experience still has a role to play in education, even when teaching a MOOC. In every case, teaching a MOOC was part of the professor's job, not a replacement. However, fame may not be the motivation and the instructor may have no desire to be the distant rock star or ship captain; rather, "what academics tend to seek is peer recognition" (Devlin, 2014). Whatever role instructors may serve when offering their expertise within future MOOCs, it will not replace the various vital roles instructors perform in higher education outside of the MOOC course or experience.

References

Alario-Hoyos, C., Pérez-Sanagustín, M., Delgado-Kloos, C., Muñoz-Organero, M., & Rodríguez-de-las-Heras, A. (2013). Analyzing the impact of built-in and external social tools in a MOOC on educational technologies. In *Scaling up learning for sustained impact.* 5-18. Heidelberg: Springer-Verlag.

Anderson, T. (2003). Getting the mix right again: An updated and theoretical rationale for interaction. *The International Review of Research in Open and Distance Learning, 4*(2). Retrieved from http://www.irrodl.org/index.php/irrodl/article/view/149/230

Bali, M. (2014). MOOC pedagogy: Gleaning good practice from existing MOOCs. MERLOT *Journal of Online Learning and Teaching, 10*(1), 44-56. Retrieved from http://jolt.merlot.org/vol10no1/bali_0314.pdf

Bonk, C. J., & Zhang, K. (2008). *Empowering online learning: 100+ activities for reading, reflecting, displaying, and doing.* San Francisco, CA: Jossey-Bass.

Berge, Z. L. (1995). Facilitating computer conferencing: Recommendations from the field. *Educational Technology, 35*(1), 22-30.

Clark, D. (2013). *Taxonomy of eight types of MOOCs.* Donald Clark Plan B Blog. Retrieved from http://donaldclarkplanb.blogspot.co.uk/2013/04/moocs-taxonomy-of-8-types-of-mooc.html

Collison, G., Elbaum, B., Haavind, S., & Tinker, R. (2000). *Facilitating online learning: strategies for moderators.* Madison: Atwood.

Conole, G. (2013). *Current thinking on the 7Cs of Learning Design.* Retrieved from http://e4innovation.com

Cormier, D., & Siemens, G. (2010). Through the open door: Open courses as research, learning, and engagement. *Educause. 45*(4), 30-39. Retrieved from http://www.educause.edu/EDUCAUSE+Review/EDUCAUSEReviewMagazineVolume45/ThroughtheOpenDoorOpenCoursesa/209320

Croxton, R. A. (2014, June). The role of interactivity in student satisfaction and persistence in online learning, *MERLOT Journal of Online Learning and Teaching, 10*(2), 314-325. Retrieved from http://jolt.merlot.org/vol10no2/croxton_0614.pdf

Davidson, C. (2013). What was the first MOOC? *A Look at MOOCs, HASTAC.* Retrieved from http://www.hastac.org/blogs/cathy-davidson/2013/09/27/what-was-first-mooc

Devlin, K. (2014, January). Matthink, mooc, v4, part 9. *MOOCTalk.* Retrieved from http://mooctalk.org/2014/01/02/maththink-mooc-v4-part-9/

Downes, S. (2005, December 22). *An introduction to connective knowledge.* [Web log posting]. Retrieved from http://www.downes.ca/cgi-bin/page.cgi?post=33034

FutureLearn. (2014). *About - FutureLearn.* Retrieved from https://www.futurelearn.com/about

Haavind, S. (2007). An interpretative model of key heuristics that promote collaborative dialogue among online learners. *Journal of Asynchronous Learning Networks, 11*(3), 39-68.

Harasim, L. (1993). *Global networks: Computers and communication.* Cambridge: MIT Press.

Hew, K. F. & Cheung, W. S. (2014). Students' and instructors' use of massive open online courses (MOOCs): Motivations and challenges, *Educational Research Review,* Volume 12, pp. 45-58. Elsevier. DOI: 10.1016/j.edurev.2014.05.001

Hiltz, S. R., & Goldman, R. (2005). *Learning together online: Research on online learning networks.* Mahwah, NJ: Lawrence Erlbaum Associates.

Hollands, F. M., & Tirthali, D. (2014, May). *MOOCs: expectations and reality. Full Report.* Center for Cost Studies of Education, Teachers College, Columbia University, N.Y. Retrieved from http://cbcse.org/wordpress/wp-content/uploads/2014/05/MOOCs_Expectations_and_Reality.pdf

Jashik, S. (2013, February 4). MOOC Mess. *Inside Higher Ed.* [Web log comment]. Retrieved from https://www.insidehighered.com/news/2013/02/04/coursera-forced-call-mooc-amid-complaints-about-course

Kirin, D., Boucher Ferguson, R., & Kirk Prentice, P. (March, 2013). Reimagining the possible with data analytics – SAS, *MIT Sloan Management Review,* Research Report, *54*(1). Retrieved from http://sloanreview.mit.edu/reports/analytics-innovation/

Kolowich, S. (2013, March 18). The professors who make the MOOCs. *Chronicle of Higher Education.* Retrieved from http://chronicle.com/article/The-Professors-Behind-the-MOOC/137905/

Liu, X., Bonk, C. J., Magjuka, R J., Lee, S. H., & Su, B. (2005). Exploring four dimensions of online instructor roles: A program level case study. *Journal of Asynchronous Learning Networks, 9*(4), 29-48.

Merriam, S. B. (1998). *Qualitative research and case study applications in education.* San Francisco: Jossey-Bass.

Moessinger, S. (2013, September 13). MOOC around the world series, part 6 moocish online educational resources. *MOOC News and Reviews* [Blog post] Retrieved from http://moocnewsandreviews.com/mooc-around-the-world-part-6-moocish-online-ed-resources/#ixzzBjlN6mXj

Nawrot, I., & Doucet, A. (2014). Building engagement for MOOC students: introducing support for time management on online learning platforms. *WWW Companion '14 Proceedings of the companion publication of the 23rd international conference on World Wide Web companion,* 1077-1082.

Perotta, C. (2014). *The digitation of knowledge produces hybrids: politics and identities in MOOCs.* Paper presented at the Networked Learning Conference 2014, Edinburgh, Scotland, 9th, April 2014.

Reeves, T. C., & Hedberg, J. G. (2014). MOOCs: Let's get REAL. *Educational Technology,* Vol. 54, No.1, 2014, 3-6.

Rohfeld, R. W., & Hiemstra, R. (1995). Moderating discussions in the electronic classroom. In Z. Berge and M. Collins (Eds.), *Computer Mediated Communication and the Online Classroom* Volume 3: Distance Learning (91-104). Cresskill NJ: Hampton Press.

Ross, J., Sinclair, C., Knox, J., Bayne, S., & Macleod, H. (2014). Teacher experiences and academic identity: The missing components of MOOC pedagogy. *MERLOT Journal of Online Learning and Teaching, 10*(1), 56-68. Retrieved from http://jolt.merlot.org/vol10no1/ross_0314.pdf

Scardamalia, M., & Bereiter, C. (1994). Computer support for knowledge-building communities. *The Journal of the Learning Sciences, 3,* 265–283.

Siemens, G. (2005, August 10). Connectivism: Learning as network creation. *e-Learning Space.org website.* Retrieved from http://www.elearnspace.org/Articles/networks.htm

Siemens, G. (2013, October 12). *MOOCs: Where next?* Keynote presentation at eLearn 2013 Preconference symposium on MOOCs and Open Education around the World, Las Vegas, NV.

Stake, R. E. (1995). *The art of case study research.* Thousand Oaks, CA: Sage.

Stake, R. E. (2008). Qualitative case studies. In N. K. Denzin, & Lincoln, Y. S. (Eds.), Strategies of Qualitative Inquiry (pp. 119-149). Los Angeles: Sage.

Swan, K., Day, S., Bogle, L., & van Prooyen, T. (2014). AMP: A tool for characterizing the pedagogical approaches of MOOCs. *e-Mentor, 2*(54), 75-85.

Tomkin, J. H., & Charlevoix, D. (2014, March). Do professors matter? Using an a/b test to evaluate the impact of instructor involvement on MOOC student outcomes. In *L@S '14: Proceedings of the first Association of Computer Machining conference on Learning @ scale,* (pp. 71-78). ACM, New York, NY, US.

Wilkowski, J., Russell, D. M., & Deutsch, A. (2014, March). Self-evaluation in advanced power searching and mapping with google MOOCs. *L@S '14: Proceedings of the first Association of Computer Machining conference on Learning @ scale* (pp. 109-116). ACM, New York, NY, US.

Yin, R. K. (1984). *Case study research: Design and methods.* Beverly Hills, CA: Sage.

Zhang, Y. (2013). Benefiting from MOOC. In Jan Herrington et al. (Eds.), *Proceedings of World Conference on Educational Multimedia, Hypermedia and Telecommunications 2013* (pp. 1372-1377). Chesapeake, VA: AACE.

Sarah Haavind is Senior Program Analyst at the Oregon Department of Education where she leads the design and implementation of a statewide online professional learning portal. She was an Associate Professor of Education at Lesley University Graduate School of Education and began her career as a high school teacher. She taught online in the 1990s for The Concord Consortium where she co-authored Facilitating Online Learning (Atwood, 2000) at Lesley University in the early 2000s, and currently adjuncts at Pepperdine University in a blended doctoral program in Learning Technologies. She can be contacted at Sarah.Haavind@pepperdine.edu.

Cynthia Sistek-Chandler is Associate Professor of Educational Technology at National University where she taught her first online class in 2000. Dr. Sistek-Chandler is currently serving a special appointment as a Faculty Fellow to the Center for Innovation and Learning, also at National University. She can be reached at cchandler@nu.edu.

International Jl. on E-Learning (2015) **14**(3) Special Issue, 351-371

Developing MOOCs to Narrow the College Readiness Gap: Challenges and Recommendations for a Writing Course

SHOBA BANDI-RAO

Borough of Manhattan Community College, CUNY, NY, USA

sbandirao@bmcc.cuny.edu

CHRISTOPHER J. DEVERS

Indiana Wesleyan University, Indiana, USA

christopherdevers@gmail.com

Massive Open Online Courses (MOOCs) have demonstrated the potential to deliver quality and cost effective course materials to large numbers of students. Approximately 60% of first-year students at community colleges are underprepared for college-level coursework. One reason for low graduation rates is the lack of the overall college readiness. MOOCs offering "remedial" writing have the potential to better prepare high school graduates for college, thereby increasing their chances of completing a degree and reducing the cost of education for students, families, institutions, and taxpayers. However, MOOCs are typically more suitable for motivated and prepared students. Designing a MOOC on writing for a diverse group of students who lack basic academic writing skills requires thoughtful modifications. In this article, we examine the needs of basic writers and the challenges involved in providing personalized feedback on the content of student writings via a MOOC platform. We recommend some MOOC variations that would be suitable for college readiness writing courses: Limited MOOC (lMOOC), Hybrid MOOC (hMOOC), Flipped MOOC (fMOOC), Mini MOOC (mMOOC), MOOC Workshops (MOOCw).

INTRODUCTION

Massive Open Online Courses (MOOC) have entered the educational space with a bang. The first MOOC was offered in 2008 by George Siemens and Stephens Downes in Canada to a couple thousand students (Downes, 2009). However, the media did not pick up on this trend until the fall of 2011 when some MOOC enrollments from Stanford University topped 100,000 participants (Pappano, 2012). MOOCs are now seen as a disruptive force in higher education (Hollands & Tirthali, 2014; Kelly, 2014). In fact, as of December 2014, three major MOOC platforms alone, Udacity, Coursera, and edX, have already enrolled about 15 million users from many countries (Shah, 2014). Needless to say, the rise of MOOCs has been phenomenal, in spite of their inherent low faculty and student contact and extremely low course completion rate, ranging between just under 1% to nearly 20% (Jordan, 2013).

Public and private academic institutions, as well as for-profit and not-for-profit organizations are investing in developing MOOC platforms. The increasing number of MOOCs has led to the creation of websites such as Class Central, which aggregate MOOC courses. As of May 2015, Class Central lists more than 2,000 courses organized by subject area, course type, and provider.

The mass appeal of a MOOC is that it is free or affordably priced, the online course materials are often of very high quality and prepared by experienced faculty and professional course developers, and any person can enroll in the course and study from home at her convenience. A MOOC class can vary in size, ranging from a few hundred participants to hundreds of thousands. Such an equalizing and democratizing system can be a big game changer in education. It is not surprising that *The New York Times* called 2012 "The Year of the MOOCs" (Pappano, 2012). Thomas Friedman goes so far as to suggest that MOOCs have the "potential to lift more people out of poverty" (2013, para. 1). Equally bold, Clay Shirky draws a parallel between MOOCs and Napster in stating that "people have learned that knowledge can be distributed or shared just like the way they distribute and share music" (2012). Clearly, MOOCs are evolving, and people think that they have the potential to transform education as well as students (Daniel, 2012).

Currently, the lack of college readiness is one of the major contributors to low graduation rates among educationally and financially disadvantaged students. Research overwhelmingly confirms that better prepared high school graduates have higher chances of succeeding academically (Bahr, 2008; Shaughnessy, 1979). For instance, a study found that 40% of students who were not in any "remedial" course completed their two-year associate's degree within eight years as opposed to only 25% of students who were in a college readiness course completed their associates within the same time period (Attewell et al., 2006). Skinner (2014) also found in his study that only six out of 275 students who were placed in a reading support group at Gordon College graduated within three years, thereby demonstrating the importance of students having the requisite literacy skills for college study.

College readiness courses are an additional expense for students, often discouraging them from pursuing their education. Those receiving financial aid want to save their funds for future credit bearing courses. Since MOOCs are cost effective, they can play a vital role in providing college readiness courses in reading, writing, and math to low-income and underprepared high school graduates enrolled in a two-year college. However, one major issue is that the completion rates on online courses for underprepared students have been low for a wide range of reasons; from students' lack of self-efficacy (Zajacova, Lynch, & Espenshade, 2005) to their inexperience in using technology (Head, 2013; Zavarella, 2008).

There appears to be some promise for implementing introductory courses online (Vaughan, 2007; Willekens & Gibson, 2010; Xu & Jaggars, 2011). Specifically, Jaggars and Xu (2010) as well as Xu and Jaggars (2011) demonstrated that hybrid courses, where students meet online and face-to-face, have shown the same completion rates as face-to-face instruction among low-income and underserved college students. Such research lends hope for MOOCs if they can offer a chance for the instructor/tutors to meet students in the classroom. Translating courses in other languages such as Spanish would also assist innumerable learners such as those originally from Latin America but now residing in the United States (Perez-Hernandez, 2014). In effect, cost-effective MOOCs, with proper supports and supplements, have the potential to narrow the college readiness gap. If successfully deployed, they can potentially increase remedial learner graduation rates, and, in the process, reduce the cost of an education for students, families, institutions, and taxpayers.

COLLEGE READINESS GAP AND THE ROLE OF COMMUNITY COLLEGES

Community Colleges play a pivotal role in providing college readiness education to around 60% of economically and academically disadvantaged students. About 44% of undergraduate students in the United States enroll at a two-year junior or community college (Miner, 2012). Around 1,655 community colleges, both private and public, provide affordable education, flexible schedules, and a host of services such as tutoring, academic and career counseling, college readiness education (U. S. Department of Education, 2005). While more than 50% of the students complete college within six years, only 25% of low-income students complete college in the same amount of time (U. S. Department of Education, NCES, 2014).

Many two-year colleges require their incoming first-year students to take placement tests in reading, writing, and math using COMPASS, ACC-UPLACER, or SAT. Those who do not pass the placement tests are required to get additional support before registering or while registered for credit courses. Community Colleges often offer college readiness education in one or more of the following ways:

1. Semester long non-credit face-to-face, hybrid, and online courses.

2. Mandated intensive tutoring while taking college-level courses.

3. Mandated pre-freshman summer enrichment session(s) offered prior to the Fall semester.

4. Cohort models where students with similar needs are placed together.

5. Short workshops that target specific topics.

6. Online self-paced modules that students are required to complete in specific problematic areas.

In addition to subject area enrichment, community colleges often provide students with a range of support services that include academic, career, health, and personal counseling, as well as academic skills workshops. These workshops include practical skills like note-taking techniques, time management seminars, study techniques, test taking skills, helpful memory techniques, working in study groups, effective listening methods, and preparing for exams. Several studies have demonstrated that these non-academic services have helped colleges improve retention and graduation rates (Lotkowski, Robbins, & Noeth, 2004; Muraskin, 1998).

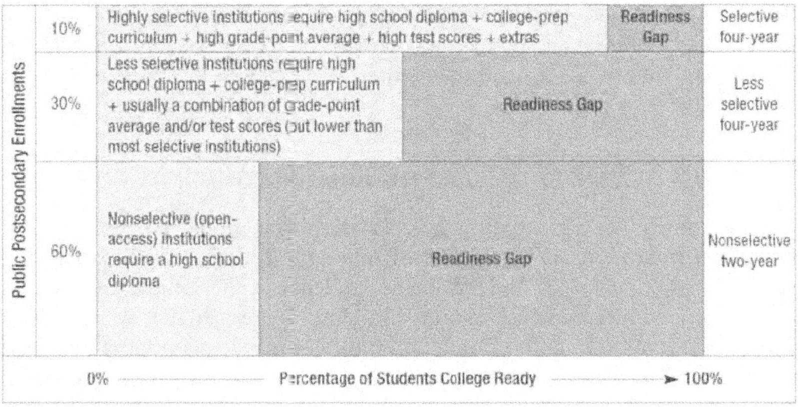

Figure 1. The readiness gap by institutional sector (The National Center for Public Policy and Higher Education (U.S.), 2013).

The college readiness gap is the largest at open access non selective two-year colleges (see Figure 1). Around 60% of high school graduates entering a community college are enrolled in one or more college readiness courses (National Center for Public Policy and Higher Education, 2013). Miner (2012) found that 55% of Hispanics and 50% of African Americans holding a degree in science or engineering have attended a community college. Clearly, community colleges play a pivotal role in providing college readiness to students to pursue and complete a degree. The National Center for Public Policy and Higher Education stresses the need for cost effective introductory or gateway courses to narrow the existing college readiness gap (Trombley & Sallo, 2012). Given such concerns combined with the confluence of trends in college affordability and budgetary cutbacks, new and improved approaches for designing, teaching, and assessing college readiness courses are needed.

Mt. San Jacinto College in California, partnering with Cousera, was among a few institutions to pilot a college readiness MOOC titled "Crafting an Effective Writer: Tools of the Trade," that was funded by the Bill and Melinda Gates Foundation. Over 40,000 students enrolled in the course and around 30,000 were active participants. Fourteen staff members were assigned to respond to student queries on the discussion board. Of the 30,000 participants, over 3,500 completed the final peer-reviewed essay; however, only 2,700 students completed the course successfully—about 6.7%. Due to the low completion rate, future offerings of the course were put on hold, as it is being reevaluated (Poulin, 2013; Whitmer, Schiorring, & James, 2014).

Several studies have found strong evidence for non-academic support services and "social presence" contributing to the success of at-risk, first-year college students (Lotkowski, Robbins, & Noeth, 2004; Muraskin, 1998). Since the online implementation of social interaction and support services has been discussed in various studies (Fowler, 2013; Grant-Vallone, Reid, Umali, & Pohlert, 2003; Jaggars, 2011; Picciano, 2002; Richardson & Swan, 2003), it is not the focus of this article. Instead, we focus on the challenges of responding to essays with personalized comments in MOOCs. In fact, we believe that such personalization and feedback issues are among the main challenges facing MOOCs that focus on basic writing or that contain extensive writing components. If the initial challenges experienced with the pilot MOOC on basic writing can be addressed, MOOCs will play a crucial role in helping thousands of low-income and underprepared high school graduates become college ready. Understanding these challenges is the first step toward designing a better MOOC on essay writing and narrowing the college readiness gap.

IMPLEMENTING MOOC FOR COLLEGE READINESS WRITING: CHALLENGES

Understanding Basic Writers and Basic Writing

Basic learners are a diverse group primarily consisting of both traditional and non-traditional students—including high school graduates who are underprepared for college-level coursework and first generation college students. The group may include students with learning difficulties, immigrants who have recently arrived in the US, students whose education has been disrupted for various reasons such as wars or political situations, and ESL learners who may lack skills in one or more subject areas. At times, students who did not take placement tests seriously and failed on it also find themselves in basic writing courses.

A majority of basic learners at community colleges are from low-income families (Terenzini, Springer, Yaeger, Pascarella, & Nora, 1996) and require additional support. Miner found that 50% of the students are Hispanic, while 45% are African American and Asian (2013). Additionally, first-generation college students are often different from traditional students in their preparation and motivation (Allen, 1999; Inman & Mayes, 1999; Terenzini et al., 1996). Specifically, they generally have lower GPAs and do not receive the same level and type of support for education from their families that students whose parents have pursued higher education do (Riehl, 1994).

Shaughnessy (1979) examined approximately four thousand essays written by community college first-year students at the City University of New York and analyzed the types of errors. Her research suggests that the errors students made were not arbitrary, as writing faculty had previously thought. Instead, the errors were based on students' lack of exposure to rules in academic writing and discourse. In effect, their writings were not in the discourse(s) expected in academia. Shaughnessy saw the writers as being intelligent, but found a serious disconnect between the knowledge and skills basic writers bring to class and the expectations of their teachers. Shaughnessy's (1979) pioneering work brought much needed attention to what has been termed "basic writing."

A variety of terms have been used to refer to the writings of students who are not college ready: remedial, developmental, fundamental, compensatory, introductory, preparatory, and academic upgrading. Several of these terms are misnomers; for instance, the term "remedial" implies deficiency (Bloom, 1995), whereas "developmental" suggests skills that have not yet been fully developed. Along these same lines, "limited" or "academic upgrading" conveys that the student is "stuck" at some level. These terms end up as labels that incoming first-year students have to confront. It is important, therefore, to examine and understand the writings of underprepared college students in an effort to avoid "oversimplifying" the diverse group of students who are often labeled as underprepared. Bloom (1995) emphasizes that names are significant because of the connotations and power they carry to influence the way people perceive an entity on a normal to abnormal continuum.

Hence we prefer the term "basic writing" or "preparatory writing" to refer to the particular writing style of the diverse group of underprepared college first-year students. The term "basic writing" allows students to be perceived as "authentic members" at their academic institutions (Barthalomae, 1985; Bernstein, 2008; Bizzell, 1986; Shaughnessy, 1994). Bartholomae (1985) and Shaughnessy (1976) advise teachers to read writings of basic learners as complex texts. And Rose (1998) urges teachers to engage their students with forms of writing that are more meaningful to the writers so that they can draw on their critical thinking skills.

The main purpose of basic writing instruction is to provide students with the "basic" understanding of written academic discourse. Rose suggests that the challenges that basic writers face have to do more with "limited opportunity to build up a rich network of discourse knowledge and strategy" than "some general difference or deficit in her ability to structure or analyze experience" (1988, p. 275). Bartholomae (1985) argues that this lack of experience with academic discourse limits basic writers from developing their voice in their writings because

> [i]t is very hard for them to take on the role, the voice, the persona of an authority whose authority is rooted in scholarship, analysis, or research. They slip, then, into a more immediately available and realizable voice of authority, the voice of a teacher giving a lesson or the voice of a parent lecturing at the dinner table. (p. 591)

Holbrook (1999) observed formulaic writing technique in GED essays and emphasizes the need for students to move away from being "writers as slaves to form" to being natural "communicators" with confidence (p. 16).

Unlike students who are fairly proficient in writing college-level essays, basic writers often struggle to satisfy the requirements set in the college composition classes. A common faux pas made in delivering instruction to basic writers is to employ the same approach used when teaching "remedial" writing. Such an approach often demoralizes the students and inhibits them from expressing their ideas freely and creatively in their writings (Shaughnessy, 1979).

It is important to distinguish basic writing from remedial writing simply because basic writers are not "deficient" as writers. It is equally important to distinguish basic writing from English as a Second Language (ESL) writing. In fact, Benson, Deming, Denzer, and Valeri-Gold (1992) stress that "it is better that English as a Second Language students and basic writers be taught by trained personnel in each area and with materials appropriate to their needs." Basic writers use a dialect of English effectively and in sophisticated ways. They mainly need exposure to formal written English, academic culture and discourse (Barthalomae, 1985; Rose, 1988). Adult ESL learners, on the other hand, have already developed essay writing skills in their first language, even though the writing style may differ based on cultural experiences. ESL learners require practice with the English language in areas such as listening, speaking, reading, writing, vocabulary, grammar, idioms, culture, etc. (Carson et al., 1990; Larsen-Freeman, 2007).

Awareness of this distinction between basic writing and ESL writing is especially important when using a MOOC platform where anyone can register for the course. For instance, in the pilot study conducted at Mt. San Jacinto College in California, Hanz found that a higher than expected number of ESL learners (about 65%) enrolled in the MOOC titled "Crafting an Effective Writer: Tools of the Trade" (Poulin, 2013). Given such findings, it is important to point out that ESL learners and basic writers have distinct linguistic needs. Because basic writers are learning to use the academic discourse, they typically require more personalized feedback on their writings delivered in a step-by-step and a structured manner (Schunk & Rice, 1993).

Providing Personalized Feedback in MOOCs

MOOC platforms initially began offering courses in the sciences. The quantitative nature of responses in the sciences lend themselves favorably to machine grading that MOOCs depend on since they enroll large numbers of students. However, MOOCs in the humanities and the social sciences have steadily increased. David Koller and Andrew Ng, co-founders of Coursera, acknowledge that in the humanities, when the response to a question is open to interpretation, automated grading systems, in their current form, have limitations (Reichard, 2013).

The qualitative nature of essay writing presents unique challenges for MOOC implementers. Based on her experience of offering a MOOC on college composition at Georgia Institute of Technology, Karen Head (2013) stated:

> For now, the technology is lacking for courses in subjects like writing, which have such strong qualitative evaluation requirements. Too often we found our pedagogical choices hindered by the course-delivery platform we were required to use, when we felt that the platform should serve the pedagogical requirements. (par. 6)

Pat James Hanz, Dean of Instruction, Library, and Technology at Mt. San Jacinto College, cautions faculty about the impossibility of grading thousands of essays without an automated essay grading system or a workable peer-assessment system (Poulin, 2013).

Two major MOOC platforms, namely edX (MIT and Harvard's non-profit organization) and Coursera (Stanford's MOOC startup), use two distinct approaches to assess essays. For example, edX makes use of an Automated Essay Scoring (AES) application, whereas Coursera uses a Calibrated Peer Review (CPR) system. Both approaches have advantages and disadvantages for evaluating essays, but not practical for basic writing.

In order for edX's scoring system to function effectively, an instructor must first score 100 student essays on one particular topic using a defined set of criteria. The machine learning algorithms then learn from the instructors' scoring patterns and use characteristics—the average length of the word, discourse element, essay, the number of words in the essay, frequency of words that are not common, scores assigned to essays with similar vocabulary—to assign a score to the essay (Balfour, 2013). One major advantage of using an AES system for a MOOC writing course, is that thousands of essays can be graded in a short span of time, and students receive a score and some feedback immediately. Another advantage is that studies have shown a high correlation between essays graded by humans and AES systems for short essays on a focused topic (Attali, 2007). Shermis et al. (2010) also found that machines graded essays were more consistent in their scoring than human graders.

Even though machine grading systems seem practical, they have come under criticism for their limitations. For instance, Yang, Buckendhal, Juszkiewicz, & Bhola (2002) stress that AES systems rely too heavily on surface features such as word, sentence, and essay length, than on the content of the essay and the creativity of the writer. Further, AES systems are unable to assess idioms, metaphors, humor, and words or phrases from a different dialect (Graesser & McNamera, 2012). Another limitation is that AES system has to be trained for each essay topic, which is an investment in time, as an instructor has to grade around 100 essays (Balfour, 2013). In addition to such problems, Ben-Simon and Benette (2007) found that psychologically, students' motivational level decreased when they learned that their writings were scored by a machine.

Coursera, on the other hand, uses a Calibrated Peer Review (CPR) system to grade essays. Students in the MOOC writing class are trained to score essays using a multiple-choice rubric, and learn the "critical points" of an essay. Next, they calibrate to an instructor's expectations on a second set of essays. Based on how well they match the instructor's score, each student receives a Reviewer Complexity Index (RCI) rating. If the RCI is very low, then students retake the test again. Each student's essay is assigned three peers to review the essay. The CPR system has a Web-based application that assigns and monitors the flow of student essays in the MOOC class. Students not only score their peers' essays, but they also evaluate their own essay. The system takes the weighted averages of all the scores and provides one final score for the essay. If there is a discrepancy between two peer reviewers, the CPR system takes the score from the student with the higher RCI (Balfour, 2013).

The advantages of using the peer-review system are that more creative pieces of writing can be evaluated and students can comment on the content of essay. Additionally, the writer feels better when she knows that the essay will be read by a person. Research studies indicate that students like the peer-review approach, as they feel they improve not only their own writing, but also gain meta-awareness about writing skills by reading peers' essays from the perspective of a reader or evaluator (Russell, 2004). Handling essays from thousands of students in a good-sized MOOC class requires a larger server for the CPR system. Since the evaluation of one essay is dependent on three other students in class, the consistency of student participation and submission of assignments has an effect on how essays are assigned for peer review. For instance, Balfour (2013) points out that an essay may be evaluated by all three students with low RCIs. Another drawback of CPR is that essays longer than 750 words can become time-consuming.

Neither AES nor CPR are suitable for basic writers because they cannot provide the kind of qualitative feedback that basic writers need. For instance, the AES system is unable to judge the quality of the essay content unless it is a highly structured "cookie cutter" five-paragraph type of essay. Assessment should not compromise on the creativity skills of the writer. Donald Murray states, "We have to respect the student, not for his product, not for the paper we call literature by giving it a grade, but for the search of truth in which he is engaged" (1972 p. 5). In addition to respecting the exploratory or creative nature of the writing process, basic writers also need to learn to write across the curriculum. By writing in different disciplines and for varying purposes, their writing skills are strengthened.

The CPR system is also not adequate to narrow the gap in college readiness because basic writers are still in the process of familiarizing themselves to the formal writing style in an academic essay. Stated another way, they are not yet in a position to provide constructive feedback to their peers even with the help of a detailed rubric. For instance, Witte and Faigley (1981) find that basic writers experience difficulty in elaborating and extending the concepts they introduce. Therefore, personalized and encouraging comments are helpful in moving the basic writer to the next level; for example, "I like your idea of using pets as a way to deal with loneliness. Earlier in your essay, you mentioned your grandfather who cannot go outside because of his physical disability. Is there a way you can connect the two and expand on the central connection?" and "Provide as much details as you can." Such constructive comments help basic writers think more critically about writing as they learn to revise their essays. Learning a new way to write takes time because writing is a process (Elbow, 1987).

Therefore, MOOCs for basic writers would require a large number of trained tutors to read, evaluate, conference, comment, and grade essays. Such requirements can not only add to the cost of the MOOC, but also add to the challenge of hiring and training large numbers of writing tutors. However, some institutions have already addressed these challenges.

For instance, the City University of New York (CUNY)—one of the largest urban campuses in the United States, consisting of 23 colleges, 11 of which are community colleges—has opted to use trained writing faculty to grade placement essays. If incoming freshmen at CUNY do not have the required passing score on the Regents or the TOEFL, they are required to complete a writing placement test, the CUNY Assessment Test in Writing (CATW) that measures the ability to read a passage and respond in writing at the college level. Around 35,000 placement tests are administered each year (Maiz, 2014). Between April 2010 and May 2014, CUNY had already trained 539 CATW certified readers (Maiz, 2014). Although training, norming, and certifying faculty can be a daunting endeavor, the benefits are far reaching.

Using trained instructors allows room for basic writers to express creativity in their writings using rich rhetorical modes, including narration, and not be restricted to highly structured essay formats. This simple shift renders writing task into more relatable, meaningful, and "authentic tasks" that provide learning opportunities from which students can benefit (Herrington, Reeves, & Oliver, 2010). Further, since the test is not machine graded, there is no limit to the number of essay prompts used, thereby protecting the quality of learning.

IMPLEMENTING MOOCS FOR BASIC WRITING: RECOMMENDATIONS

Implementing a MOOC on writing for college underprepared students presents some challenges. But in these challenges, we also see opportunities for a variety of hybrid-type MOOCs for teaching basic writing, where students interface with faculty from time to time. Below we detail five types of MOOCs that educators may want to consider, including the Limited MOOC (lMOOC), Hybrid MOOC (hMOOC), Flipped MOOC (fMOOC), Mini MOOC (mMOOC), and MOOC Workshop (MOOCw).

Limited MOOC or lMOOC

The juxtaposition of the terms "limited" and "massive" may seem like an oxymoron, but from the perspective of a first-year composition class, 2,000 to 4,000 students in one course is massive. At many colleges, a traditional basic writing class is generally limited to 20 to 25 students per section; which is small in comparison to the large lecture classes in other fields with hundreds of students.

The enrollment in a lMOOC is limited by a preset number and to individual institutions for two reasons: (1) in order to have a manageable number of trained writing tutors who can conference with students individually, address specific needs more effectively, and provide appropriate feedback on the students writings; and (2) to ensure that only basic writers are enrolled in the course. Many two-year colleges have in place some sort of criteria that channels ESL students into ESL writing courses and basic writers into "remedial" or "developmental" writing courses.

In a lMOOC course, students watch video lectures online, read select-ed texts/essays, discuss them online with their peers in small and/or large groups, complete reading comprehension tasks/exercises, etc. As students draft their own essays, each writer meets with her tutor to discuss and re-ceive feedback. The tutor and the student could conference face-to-face or online via Skype or Google+ Hangouts for synchronous sessions. Applica-tions such as screencast-o-matic or track changes on Word could also be used for asynchronous feedback. We recommend synchronous sessions for initial drafts and the asynchronous for later drafts. Writing drafts, receiving personalized feedback and encouraging comments are essential to the ba-sic writing class because they help guide basic writers through the expecta-tions of academic writing. Given that the course materials are online, stu-dents have the flexibility to study anytime, anywhere, making it convenient for working students or a stay-at-home parent with kids. Before the course begins, we encourage institutions to provide workshops for students to be-come familiar with the various features of the online platform.

Since the lMOOC requires a large number of tutors (between 50 and 80 tutors for a course with 2,000 students), there will be additional costs for training tutors and for having individual sessions with students. Each tutor would work with 25 to 40 students a semester. This cost could be covered by having students pay a minimal fee for the personalized feedback they receive on three to four essays during the semester. Institutions can also find ways to subsidize or waive the fees for students who need financial assis-tance. Although there is a small cost, lMOOCs will still be less expensive than what students would pay for a typical semester-long course.

Hybrid MOOC or hMOOC

A hMOOC is another way to implement semester-long basic writing course. Instead of meeting regularly in the classroom, students work most-ly online, but also meet with the faculty face-to-face from time-to-time in the classroom. A hMOOC can be limited to the regular basic writing class-size (namely 20-25 students) or to several sections of basic writing classes grouped together. In a large hMOOC, however, several instructors are need-ed to meet with small groups of students in person on campus or at learning hubs. Coursera, for instance, is currently partnering with the New York City Public Library on a pilot study using libraries as a "learning hub," where trained facilitators meet small groups of students face-to-face several times during the semester (Coursera Blog, 2014).

As in lMOOCs, students in the hMOOC also view video lectures, read articles/essays, and discuss with classmates online. However, in the hMOOC, students do not have tutors to provide one-on-one help as they draft and write their essays. Instead, students meet with a faculty in small groups a few times during the semester on campus. Activities may include peer-reviewing a student-essay as a group where the facilitator guides students as they review and revise the essay. Students then apply these skills to revise and edit their own essays at home.

Most community colleges require their students to take two English composition courses in their freshman year. The hMOOC would ideal for basic writers taking their second English composition course; that is, for students who have had some prior experience in writing an academic college essay upon completing their first English composition course, in class, or via a fMOOC (see below) or a lMOOC. Although the hMOOC provides flexibility for community college students who hold jobs, we recommend it for students who are highly motivated as a lot of the online course work has to be done independently. We also recommend that institutions provide adequate training to students to use the online platform efficiently.

Blended classrooms provide a nice balance between online and face-to-face discussions. Meeting small groups in person are helpful as basic writers rely heavily on "verbal and nonverbal communication techniques" from the teacher and peers to gain assurance in their work (Balmuth, 1986). Additionally, personal contact from time to time encourages students to stay on course and complete it.

Sorden and Munene (2013) found that students in blended classes reported to be satisfied with the course due to the social presence and collaborative activities. We recommend that hMOOCs implement collaborative activities and ensure a good social presence online. Bonk and Khoo (2014), in their book, *Adding some TEC-VARIETY: 100+ Activities for Motivating and Retaining Learners Online*, provide several tips and suggestions for enhancing teaching and learning to motivate students and teachers and increase retention in the online courses.

Flipped MOOC or fMOOC

In the fMOOC, basic writers meet with their instructor regularly in class during its scheduled hours. However, instead of listening to lectures in class, students watch the video lectures online as part of their homework. The class time, instead, is used for students to discuss and conference with their instructor.

Flipping classwork and homework allows basic writers to have quality time to interact with the instructor in the classroom. Although fMOOC seems like an ideal platform for basic writers, we recommend fMOOC for basic writers who are mature, disciplined, and motivated since the success of the course depends on students doing their homework regularly and coming prepared to class.

Since the size of the fMOOC is limited to the usual class size at the community college, it is not any more cost effective than the regular classes. The advantage, however, is that students can get more one-on-one quality time and feedback from their classroom instructor.

Mini MOOC or mMOOC

A mMOOC is short course lasting anywhere between three and six weeks. mMOOC addresses one or two specific aspects of basic writing. Basic writers tend to learn new information better when it is presented in small manageable chunks (Bandi-Rao, 2013). In a mMOOC course, basic learners are exposed to well-written student essays that serve as authentic models of college writing, academic discourse, and culture. Reading of each sample essay is followed by multiple choice questions that direct the student's attention to various aspects of expository writing—audience, ideas, organization, arguments, evidence, transitions, coherence, formal language, vocabulary, etc. These sample essays progress from simple narratives to more complex rhetorical modes. A similar course can be offered on critical reading and critical thinking.

Since the exercises are mostly multiple-choice, they can be machine graded, which in turn, allows any number of writers, not just basic writers, across community colleges in the United States to enroll. Students are more engaged when they receive immediate feedback on their exercises and tests.

The short duration of a mMOOC has the potential to decrease the drop-out rates that semester-long MOOCs currently experience. In addition to giving students a sense of accomplishment, they also provide basic learners an idea of what a semester-long MOOC entails. As in the previous MOOCs mentioned, the mMOOC is also limited to basic writers. However, in the mMOOC, basic writers from other two-year colleges can also enroll in the course.

MOOC Workshops or MOOCw

MOOCw is a weekend workshop that covers one or two peripheral components of academic writing (e.g., avoiding plagiarism, overcoming writer's block, using common punctuations correctly, MLA format, etc.). Addressing peripheral topics separately allows the classroom instructor to maintain focus on essay writing as basic writers can work on these writing components at their own convenience. Since these peripheral components are general, anyone can enroll in this workshop.

As in the mMOOC, students watch video lectures, read examples, work on practice exercises, discuss on a group forum, and take a test at the end. Since the responses to questions are quantitative in nature, students receive immediate feedback as the tests are machine graded.

Students enroll in a specific MOOCw on a need basis or on the recommendation of the instructor from a semester long MOOC. Because MOOCw is a short workshop, students would be more likely to commit to it. As students learn new information in small steps, they gain confidence by mastering one step at a time.

Below is a table that presents the key distinguishing features for each of the five variations of MOOCs discussed above.

Table 1

Comparison of the key features of the five MOOCs recommended for basic writers

	IMOOC (limited MOOC)	hMOOOC (hybrid MOOC)	fMOOC (flipped MOOC)	mMOOC (mini MOOC)	MOOCw (MOOC workshop)
Duration	semester	semester	semester	2 to 6 weeks	weekend
Online/ Hybrid	hybrid	hybrid	hybrid	online	online
Class size	limited	limited	limited	limited	not limited
Content	academic essay writing for basic writers	academic essay writing for basic writers	academic essay writing for basic writers	academic literacy skills for basic writers (e.g., critical writing, reading, and thinking)	review topics about academic writing (e.g., plagiarism, overcoming writer's block, MLA format)
Advantages	• personalized feedback from trained tutors • addresses needs of basic writers	• small group meetings with instructor in person • addresses needs of basic writers	• personalized feedback from instructor • quality time with instructor in class • addresses needs of basic writers	• immediate feedback (computer graded) • addresses needs of basic writers • duration of course	• immediate feedback (computer graded) • enrollment open for anyone • duration of course
Dis-advantages	• additional cost for a large number of tutors • course limited to basic writers within individual colleges	• coordinate group meetings on campus or at learning hubs • course limited to basic writers within individual colleges	• identifying basic writers who have sufficient self-efficacy and motivation	• no personalized feedback • course limited to basic writers from any two-year college	• no personalized feedback

CONCLUSION

Many high-school graduates are underprepared for college, and MOOCs offer one avenue to help close the college readiness gap. President Barak Obama, in his 2009 American Graduation Initiative, draws attention to the significant role community colleges will play in educating and preparing students for future jobs; "Earning a post-secondary degree or credential is no longer just a pathway to opportunity for a talented few; rather, it is a prerequisite for the growing jobs of the new economy" ("Higher Education. The White House," n.d.). President Obama's goal is to increase graduation rates at community colleges by 5 million by 2020 ("Higher Education. The White House," n.d). Without a doubt, new and improved approaches for designing, teaching, and assessing college readiness courses have become the need of the hour. Community colleges now have to face the challenge of providing access while maintaining the quality of learning (Perin, 2006).

Arguably, MOOCs are successful at providing free (or low cost) education. However, they are not well suited for courses that require personalized feedback, such as a course for basic writers. Given what we have learned about MOOC education in the past few years, we are starting to see changes taking place that address specific learner needs. For instance, Professor Auh Yoon-il of Kyung Hee Cyber University in Seoul, Korea proposed the "one culture MOOC" or ocMOOC in Korea in an attempt to have a more homogenous student population (Park, 2014). He suggests that when this occurs, the course content can be fine-tuned and made more meaningful to the students. An ocMOOC, in turn, may increase the retention and completion rates for students. Similarly, we proposed five unique MOOCs that could be valuable for basic writers; namely, (1) lMOOC, (2) hMOOC, (3) fMOOC, (4) mMOOC, and (5) MOOCw.

Given the unique needs of the basic writers, current MOOCs are not beneficial in developing their writing skills. However, the five specialized MOOCs that we propose offer the frameworks and supports that basic writers need. Overall, past literature and data on basic writing offer a strong foundation on how to design and operate MOOCs that meet the needs of specific populations or groups of learners.

References

Allen, D. (1999). Desire to finish college: An empirical link between motivation and per-sistence. *Research in Higher Education, 40*(4), 461-485.

Attali, Y. (2007). On-the-fly customization of automated essay scoring (RR-07-42). Princeton, NJ: ETS Research & Development. Retrieved from http://www.ets.org/Media/Research/pdf/RR-07-42.pdf

Attewell, P., Lavin, D., Domina, T., & Levey, T. (2006). New evidence on college remediation. *Journal of Higher Education, 77,* 886-924.

Bahr, P. R. (2008). Does mathematics remediation work? A comparative analysis of academic attainment among community college students. *Research in Higher Education, 49,* 420–450.

Balfour, S. P. (2013). Assessing writing in MOOCS: Automated essay scoring and Calibrated Peer Review. *Research & Practice in Assessment, 8*(1), 40-48.

Balmuth, M. (1986). Essential characteristics of effective adult literacy programs: A review and analysis of the research. *The Adult Beginning Reader Project.* New York: NY State Department of Education.

Bandi-Rao, S. (2013). Using M technology with ESL learners in the community college setting. *Proceedings of the Society for Information Technology & Teacher Education International Conference* (pp. 3653-3653). Chesapeake, VA: AACE.

Bartholomae, D. (1985). Inventing the university. In M. Rose (Ed.), *When a writer can't write* (pp. 134-164). New York: Guilford.

Ben-Simon, A., & Bennett, R. E. (2007). Toward more substantively meaningful automated essay scoring. *The Journal of Technology, Learning and Assessment, 6*(1).

Benson, B., Deming, M., Denzer, D., & Valeri-Gold, M. (1992). A combined basic writing/English as a second language class: Melting pot or mishmash. *Journal of Basic Writing, 11*(1), 58-59.

Bernstein, S. N. (2008). Social justice initiative for basic writing. *BWe: Basic Writing e-Journal, 7.*

Bizzell, P. (1986). What happens when basic writers come to college? *College Composition and Communication,* 294-301.

Bloom, L. (1995). A name with a view. *Journal of Basic Writing, 14*(1), 7–14.

Bonk, C. J., & Khoo, E. (2014). *Adding some TEC-VARIETY: 100+ activities for motivating and retaining learners online.* OpenWorldBooks and Amazon CreateSpace. Retrieved from http://tec-variety.com/TEC-Variety_ch3.pdf

Carson, J. E., Carrell, P. L., Silberstein, S., Kroll, B., & Kuehn, P. A. (1990). Reading writing relationships in first and second language. *TESOL Quarterly, 24*(2), 245-266.

Coursera Blog (2014, April 30). New learning hubs locations hosted by the New York Public Library and seven other international partners. *Coursera Blog.* Retrieved from http://blog.coursera.org/post/84322385012/new-learning-hubs-locations-hosted-by-the-new-york

Daniel, J. (2012). Making sense of MOOCs: Musings in a maze of myth, paradox and possibility. *Journal of Interactive Media in Education, 3.* Retrieved from http://www.jime.open.ac.uk/jime/article/viewArticle/2012-18/html/

Downes, S. (2009). The role of open educational resources in personal learning. *Open Educational Resources: Innovation, Research and Practice,* 207.

Elbow, P. (1987). The pleasures of voices in the literary essay: Explorations in the prose of Gretel Ehrlich and Richard Selzer. In C. Anderson (Ed.), *Literary nonfiction: Theory, criticism, pedagogy* (pp. 211-34). Carbondale: Southern Illinois University Press.

Fowler, G. A. (2013, October 8). An early report card on MOOCs. *Wall Street Journal.* Retrieved from http://online.wsj.com/news/articles/SB10001424052702303759604579093400834738972

Friedman, T. (2013, January 6). Revolution hits the universities. *The New York Times.* Retrieved from http://www.nytimes.com/2013/01/27/opinion/sunday/friedman-revolution-hits-the-universities.html?

Grant-Vallone, E., Reid, K., Umali, C., & Pohlert, E. (2003). An analysis of the effects of self-esteem, social support, and participation in student support services on students' adjustment and commitment to college. *Journal of College Student Retention: Research, Theory and Practice, 5*(3), 255-274.

Graesser, A. C., & McNamara, D. S. (2012). Automated analysis of essays and open-ended verbal responses. In H. Cooper, P. M. Camic, D. L. Long, A. T. Panter, D. Rindskopf, & K. J. Sher (Eds.), *APA handbook of research methods in psychology,* Vol 1: Foundations, planning, measures, and psychometrics (pp. 307-325). Washington,DC: American Psychological Association.

Head, K. (2013). Lessons learned from a freshman-composition MOOC. *The Chronicle of Higher Education.* Retrieved from http://chronicle.com/blogs/wiredcampus/lessons-learned-from-a-freshman-composition-mooc/46337?cid=wc&utm_source=wc&utm_medium=en

Herrington, J., Reeves, T. C., & Oliver, R. (2010). A guide to authentic e-learning. Routledge. "Higher Education." The White House. (n.d.). *The White House: Higher Education.* Retrieved from http://www.whitehouse.gov/issues/education/higher-education

Holbrook, A. (1999). Formulaic writing: Blueprint for mediocrity: GED. *Items, 3* (4), 8-9.

Hollands, F. M., & Tirthali, D. (2014, May). *MOOCs: Expectations and reality. Center for Benefit-Cost Studies in Education.* Teaching College, Columbia. Retrieved from http://cbcse.org/wordpress/wp-content/uploads/2014/05/MOOCs_Expectations_and_Reality.pdf

Inman, W. E., & Mayes, L. (1999). The importance of being first: Unique characteristics of first generation community college students. *Community College Review, 26*(4), 3-22.

Jaggars, S. S. (2011). *Online learning: Does it help low-income and underprepared students?* CCRC Working Paper No. 26. Assessment of Evidence Series. New York: Community College Research Center, Columbia University.

Jaggars, S. S., & Xu, D. (2010). Online Learning in the Virginia Community College System. Community College Research Center, Teachers College, Columbia University. Retrieved from http://academiccommons.columbia.edu/catalog/ac:172174

Jordan, K. (2014) Initial trends in enrolment and completion of massive open online courses. *The International Review of Research in Open and Distance Learning, 15*(1), 133-160.

Kelly, A. P. (2014, May). *Disruptor, distractor, or what?: A Policymaker's Guide to Massive Open Online Courses (MOOCs).* Bellweather Education. Retrieved from http://bellwethereducation.org/sites/default/files/BW_MOOC_Final.pdf

Larsen-Freeman, D. (2007). Reflecting on the cognitive–social debate in second language acquisition. *The Modern Language Journal, 91*(s1), 773-787.

Lotkowski, V. A., Robbins, S. B., & Noeth, R. J. (2004). The role of academic and non-academic factors in improving college retention. ACT Policy Report. (ERIC Document Reproduction Service no. ED485476).

M. Maiz, personal communication, May 24, 2014.

M. Maiz, personal communication, September 24, 2014.

Miner, J. C. (2012). America's Community Colleges. *Science, 335*(6075), 1409-1409.

Muraskin, L. D. (1998). A structured freshman year for at-risk students. *ERIC Document ED420265.* Retrieved from http://eric.ed.gov/?id=ED420265

Murray, D. (1972). Teach writing as a process not product." In Villanueva, V. (Ed) (2003). *Cross-Talk in Comp Theory: A Reader. Revised and Updated. National Council of Teachers of English.* Urbana, IL. National Council of Teachers.

The National Center for Public Policy and Higher Education (2013). *Beyond the rhetoric: Improving college readiness through coherent state policy.* Retrieved from http://www.highereducation.org/reports/college_readiness/gap.shtml

Pappano, L. (2012, November 2). The year of the MOOC. *The New York Times.* Retrieved from http://www.nytimes.com/2012/11/04/education/edlife/massive-open-online-courses-are-multiplying-at-a-rapid-pace.html?pagewanted=all&_r=0

Park, S.-m. (2014, May 31). Revolutionizing online education. *Korea Joongang Daily.* Retrieved from http://koreajoongangdaily.joins.com/news/article/article.aspx?aid=2989930

Perez-Hernandez, D. (2014, April 29). Coursera seeks to create a 'global translator community.' The Chronicle of Higher Education. Retrieved from http://chronicle.com/blogs/wiredcampus/coursera-seeks-to-create-a-global-translator-community/52129?cid=pm&utm_source=pm&utm_medium=en

Perin, D. (2006). Can community colleges protect both access and standards? The problem of remediation. *Teachers College Record, 108*(3), 339-373.

Picciano, A. G. (2002). Beyond student perceptions: Issues of interaction, presence, and performance in an online course. *Journal of Asynchronous Learning Networks, 6*(1), 21–40.

Poulin, R. (2013, September 21). Crafting an effective MOOC: One community college's experience. *WCET Frontiers.* Retrieved from http://wcetblog.wordpress.com/2013/08/06/creating-an-effective-mooc/

Reichard, C. (2013, June 4). MOOCs face challenges in teaching humanities. *The Stanford Daily.* Retrieved from http://www.stanforddaily.com/2013/06/04/moocs-face-challenges-in-teaching-humanities/

Richardson, J. C., & Swan, K. (2003). Examining social presence in online courses in relation to students' perceived learning and satisfaction. *Journal of Asynchronous Learning Networks, 7*(1), 68–88.

Riehl, R. J. (1994).The academic preparation, aspirations, and first-year performance of first-generation students. *College and University, 70*(1), 14-19.

Rose, M. (1988). Narrowing the mind and page: Remedial writers and cognitive reductionism. *College Composition and Communication, 39*(3), 267-302.

Russell, A. A. (2004). Calibrated peer review-a writing and critical-thinking instructional tool. *Teaching Tips: Innovations in Undergraduate Science Instruction,* 54.

Schunk, D. H., & Rice, J. M. (1993). Strategy fading and progress feedback effects on self-efficacy and comprehension among students receiving remedial reading services. *The Journal of Special Education, 27*(3), 257-276.

Shah, D. (2014). MOOCs in 2014: Breaking down the numbers. *edSurge.* Retrieved from https://www.edsurge.com/n/2014-12-26-moocs-in-2014-breaking-down-the-numbersSurge

Shaughnessy, M. P. (1976). Diving in: An introduction to basic writing. *College Composition and Communication, 27*(3), 234-239.

Shaughnessy, M. (1979). *Errors and expectations: A guide for the teacher of basic writing.* New York: Oxford University Press.

Shaughnessy, M. (1994). Some new approaches toward teaching. *Journal of Basic Writing, 13*(1), 3-16.

Shermis, M. D., Burstein, J., Higgins, D., & Zechner, K. (2010). Automated essay scoring: Writing assessment and instruction. In E. Baker, B. McGaw, & N.S. Petersen (Eds.), *International encyclopedia of education* (3rd ed., pp. 75–80). Oxford, England: Elsevier.

Shirky, C. (2012, November 12). Napster, Udacity, and the academy. *Clay Shirky*. Retrieved from http://www.shirky.com/weblog/2012/11/

Skinner, A. D. (2014). Academic outcomes among a sample of learning support community college students. *Community College Journal of Research & Practice, 38*(1), 50-53.

Sorden. S. D., & Munene, I. I. (2013). Constructs related to community college student satisfaction in blended learning. *Journal of Information Technology Education: Research, 12*, 251-270. Retrieved from http://www.jite.org/documents/Vol12/JITE-v12ResearchP251-270Sorden1206.pdf

Terenzini, P. T., Springer, L., Yaeger, P. M., Pascarella, E. T., & Nora, A. (1996). First-generation college students: Characteristics, experiences, and cognitive development. *Research in Higher education, 37*(1), 1-22.

Trombley, W. H., & Sallo, T. (2012). *American higher education: Journalistic and policy perspectives from National CrossTalk*. National Center for Public Policy and Higher Education. Retrieved from http://www.highereducation.org/crosstalk/ctbook/pdf-book/CrossTalkBook.pdf

U. S. Department of Education. (2005). *Community college facts at a glance*. (2005, October 25). Retrieved from http://www2.ed.gov/about/offices/list/ovae/pi/cclo/ccfacts.html

U.S. Department of Education, National Center for Education Statistics. (2014). The Condition of Education 2014 (NCES 2014-083),Institutional Retention and Graduation Rates for Undergraduate Students.

Vaughan, N. (2007). Perspectives on blended learning in higher education. *International Journal on E-learning, 6*(1), 81-94.

Whitmer, J., Schiorring, E., & James, P. (2014, March). Patterns of persistence: What engages students in a remedial English writing MOOC? *Proceedings of the Fourth International Conference on Learning Analytics and Knowledge* (pp. 279-280). Chesapeake, VA: AACE.

Willekens, R., & Gibson, P. (2010). Hybrid courses and student engagement: opportunities and challenges for community college leaders. *International Journal of Educational Leadership Preparation, 5*(1).

Witte, S. P., & Faigley, L. (1981). Coherence, cohesion, and writing quality. *College composition and communication, 32*, 189-204.

Xu, D., & Jaggars, S. S. (2011). *Online and hybrid course enrollment and performance in Washington State Community and Technical Colleges*. CCRC Working Paper No. 31. New York: Community College Research Center, Columbia University.

Yang, Y, Buckenthal, C. W., Juszkiewicz, P. J., & Bhola, D.S. (2002). A review of strategies for validating computer-automated scoring. *Applied Measurement in Education, 15*(4), 391-412.

Zajacova, A., Lynch, S. M., & Espenshade, T. J. (2005). Self-efficacy, stress, and academic success in college. *Research in Higher Education, 46*(6), 677-706.

Zavarella, C. A. (2008). *Computer-based instruction and remedial mathematics: A study of student retention at a Florida Community College* (Unpublished doctoral dissertation). University of South Florida, Tampa, FL. Available at ProQuest Dissertations and Theses database. (UMI No. 3326039).

Shoba Bandi-Rao is an assistant professor at the Borough of Manhattan Community College, CUNY, where she teaches *Language and Culture*, a course in linguistics and *Intensive Writing* to underprepared college freshmen. Her research focuses on ways to use technology and the appropriate pedagogical strategies to narrow the college readiness gap for disadvantaged students at two-year colleges. Currently, she is working on three projects: (1) digital storytelling as a way to help struggling writers; (2) use of small "chunks" of time and the convenience of mobile technology to practice language skills; and (3) videos created by students on academic literacy skills. She has also been keenly following the evolution of MOOCs on basic writing. Bandi-Rao received her Ph. D. in Applied Linguistics/TESOL from New York University. During her free time, she dabbles in amateur astronomy. Bandi-Rao can be contacted at sbandirao@bmcc.cuny.edu.

Christopher Devers received a Ph.D. in curriculum and instruction from the University of Illinois at Urbana-Champaign. He is an Associate Professor in the School of Education and the Director of Research for the Center for Learning and Innovation at Indiana Wesleyan University. Broadly, Professor Devers' research focuses on how and when technology promotes learning. Specifically, his research explores the optimal components that impact learning and matching those to the right situations. Overall, the broader questions regarding how and when technology is effective are applied to Professor Devers' lines of research—online education, online video learning, and the scholarship of teaching and learning. Chris can be contacted at christopherdevers@gmail.com.

International Jl. on E-Learning (2015) **14**(3) Special Issue, 373-383

Much aMOOC about Nothing:
Is Real Research Coming?

VICKI SLOAN WILLIAMS
The Pennsylvania State University, USA
vqw@psu.edu

NAI-FEN SU
The Pennsylvania State University, USA
nzs5134@psu.edu

In this age of continual technology advances, educators have become somewhat used to rapid innovation and change brought on by new learning technologies. Higher education institutions are constantly researching new forms of educational delivery, but academe in general has had some difficulty understanding the potential of MOOCs. To date, serious research on the impact of MOOCs on learning is fairly scarce. The authors examine the present state of MOOC research and speculate on why it is so.

WHERE'S THE RESEARCH?

MOOCs are a major buzzword in education today, but why is there so much attention to this phenomenon? Massively Open Online Courses or MOOCs are a hot topic, but what do we really know about them and where is that information found? How much genuine and needed research on MOOCs is being done? Where are the findings about learning analytics and MOOC student success? Has anyone shown that massive social media is really directly related to learning? How much control and structure in a MOOC is required by learners in order to meet desired outcomes?

Online learning took years to be accepted as a viable learning delivery system. During the past two decades, volumes of research have been written on the variables and factors influencing effective learning-at-a-distance.

Compared to the press on MOOCs today, few people were excited about the open educational possibilities brought about since the 1960s from the Open University in the UK and other open universities established since that time (e.g., the Open University of the Philippines, the Open University of Israel, the Korea National Open University, etc.).

For much of the last few decades, the nature of distance learning research has been more about the technical learning environment created for remote students than about how the teaching strategies that affected learning online or via television or correspondence. Another issue concerned the number of students being served in an online course. Instructors felt that teaching online was much more work than teaching a traditional face-to-face course and 30 students in an online course was the upper limit for an effective learning environment (Cavanaugh, 2005; Davidson-Shivers, 2009). In a face-to-face situation or residential course, instructors could just dust off their lecture notes and "walk" into class. This convenience was no longer possible online. To make matters worse, online education was difficult to research and calculate any sense of return on investment (ROI) for an online course. Then suddenly MOOCs appeared which could accommodate hundreds, maybe even thousands or hundreds of thousands, of students. The increased through-put affords many instructional as well as research possibilities.

THE RISE OF THE MOOC

A few years ago, the only massive online activities concerned multi-player games. There was much news about massively multi-player online games (MMOGs) and their impact on the gaming crowd (Bonk & Dennen, 2005). The idea of thousands of strangers logging on to confront one another and compete was impressive and novel, but it was perceived as having limited educational applications. Most were "just games." Until recently (Gaudiosi, 2008; Hernandez, 2014), there was just the occasional instructor who used *World of Warcraft* to teach leadership skills (Harper, 2007) or the United States recruiting game, *Go Army* (http://www.goarmy.com/downloads/games.html). Then a few folks, such as George Siemens and Dave Cormier (Cormier & Siemens, 2010) got the idea to try massively online instruction… and it caught on like wildfire.

However, in 2011, MOOCs suddenly became a hot topic. Here a MOOC, there a MOOC, everywhere a MOOC MOOC. Everybody was jumping on the bandwagon, and, eventually, the questions of "profit" and "credit" began to be raised. Many people questioned the feasibility of MOOCs as a business plan for higher education (Marshall, 2013; Meyer, 2013). MOOCs were deemed idealistic. How much could institutions of higher learning engage in altruistic practices? If MOOCs were, in fact, "Open" courses, who would pay for developing them? If these were "Open" courses, how does someone prove that he took and successfully completed it? Can a student get traditional academic credit for taking a MOOC or some form of alternative credit? How will student work be graded? Who will grant that credit and who will accept it in transfer? The questions surrounding MOOCs are seemingly endless (Daniel, 2012; Savenjie, 2012).

Some university faculty members and administrators argued that MOOCs were not real courses and those taking them did not deserve course credits (Joseph & Nath, 2013; Rajabi & Virkus, 2013). Business offices attempted to design business models to accommodate the new potential income source like Udacity, Coursera, and edX, which partner with schools or instructors to offer these courses (Korn & Levitz, 2013). Nontraditional students everywhere thought MOOCs were a new opportunity to learn without the bother of going through an admissions process and paying application fees as well as huge tuition bills (Yuan & Powell, 2013).

The media jumped all over the educational innovation, but very few were doing any real research on learning outcomes and the MOOC learning environment. Some collected information on persistence (Breslow, Pritchard, DeBoer, Stump, Ho, & Seaton, 2013), the number of hours MOOC students spent online, and how many posts they made in a discussion (Ifenthaler & Widanapathirana, 2014). Instructors measured time-on-task and employed peer-review to ease the workload, but not much empirical research was available for administrators, educators, or politicians to review on the real impact a MOOC environment had on learning.

WHAT THE LITERATURE SAYS ABOUT MOOCS IN GENERAL

In a 2013 article in open access journal, *The International Review of Research In Open and Distance Learning (IRRODL)*, Liyanagunawardena, Adams, and Williams (2013) did an extensive literature review of research published between 2008 and 2012. Using the search terms "MOOC," "massively open online course," and "massive open online course" with the journals *British Journal of Educational Technology, Distance Education, American Journal of Distance Education*, and *Journal of Online Learning and Teaching*, they found only 16 articles on MOOC research. They followed up that search with database searches in ISI Web of Knowledge and found 2 relevant articles. In addition, they retrieved 6 articles from ProQuest. In JSTOR, however, the search came up empty. In IEEEXplorer, they discovered one MOOC research article, whereas a search in Scopus generated 12 relevant articles. Across all their sources, they found fewer than 70 articles in total for the five years span that they studied. Liyanagunawardena et al. (2013) concluded:

> MOOCs have created wide interest as a change agent in higher education, and the peer-reviewed research literature on them is growing but still limited. Many articles published to date have discussed empirical evidence from case studies, the influence on higher education structure, or educational theory relating to MOOCs. While there is research into the learner perspective, neither the creator/facilitator perspective nor the technological aspects are being widely researched (or at least such research has not yet been published). MOOCs generate a plethora of data in digital form for interested researchers. However, this volume has so far limited researchers to analysing only a tiny portion of the available data, restricting our understanding of MOOCs. There are further interesting research avenues such as cultural tensions within courses and the ethical aspects of using data generated by MOOC participants still to be explored. (Liyanagunawardena, et al., 2013, p. 219)

Interested in what had taken place in terms of MOOC research since 2012, at the end of August 2013, the authors conducted a ProQuest database search on only the word "MOOC" and it turned up 1,132 results. More than 1,700 historical newspaper entries were not included. Also excluded were non-searchable digital scans dating from before 2008 as well as articles that were not relevant. As shown in Table 1, the relevant entries, sorted by ProQuest into publication categories, consisted of a variety of publication outlets (Williams, 2014).

Even after eliminating the completely irrelevant citations and mere mentions of MOOCs, 720 MOOC citations remained. At first glance, that might seem impressive for an instructional technology topic that had just emerged. However, the majority of the items covered disputes within the higher education community and editorials/opinion pieces on whether MOOCs were even worthy of the attention of institutions of higher learning.

Faculty instructors who saw the value of MOOCs as instruction for the masses argued with faculty colleagues and other educators and administrators who believed there was limited, if any, value in online courses offered to thousands of students in a single class. *Information Week's* Keith Fowlkes (2013), reported a Stanford statistics professor as saying "I don't think you can get a Stanford education online, just as I don't think that Facebook gives you a social life" (Is This All Bad? section, para. 5). In that same article, a professor at Northeastern's College of Professional Studies stated that, "The whole MOOC thing is mass psychosis. [It's] just throwing spaghetti against the wall to see what sticks" (Will MOOCs Stick? section, para. 1). Similarly, in *The Chronicle Review*, a faculty member from Youngstown State University was not optimistic about the effect MOOCs would have on smaller institutions, "...we would be forced to further reduce the number of tenure-track faculty positions and/or compensation to current faculty members as a result" (Sumell, 2013, para. 6).

Table 1

Number of MOOC Articles by Publication Category

Number of publications found in		MOOC
Conference papers		6
Dissertations		212
Government publications		9
Newspapers (online & print)		103
Newswire feeds		155
Scholarly journals		198
Trade journals		335
Working papers		3
Other periodicals		111
	Total	1,132

Other instructors and administrators wrangled over workloads and whether or not a MOOC student should be granted credit for successful completion and just WHAT even constitutes a "successful completion" (Holter, 2013). How does one assess and grade thousands of students in a single course and what does that grade really mean? There were discussions of whether or not MOOCs should be free. Such discussions led to debates about the perceived value of a "free" course (Rajab & Virkus, 2013).

Those in corporate settings as well as in higher education argued about the best business models for MOOCs (Saltzman, 2014). There was a citation in the *Bulletin of the American Society for Information Science and Technology* about a team who received a grant to produce high-quality massive open online (MOOC) data management instructional courses (Anonymous, 2013), but it included only an announcement of the grant and no project details or specifics.

At least 37 articles about MOOCs were from *Information Week* (a trade journal) and 21 were from the McClatchy-Tribune News. Of the more than 1,000 articles originally discovered, only 199 of them were from "scholarly journals" and academic publications. Of those, 80 were from *The Chronicle of Higher Education* and many were simply announcements or descriptions of what MOOC was released by what institution, including casual news regarding institutions which had just signed a partnership with Coursera or edX or others.

As these details unfolded, one could only surmise that minimal research was being conducted on the learning effectiveness of MOOCs. Even the Compendium of MOOC articles (published by EDUCAUSE's Center for Applied Research) included articles on MOOC revenue models, completion rates, and student profiling (Pirani, 2013). Unfortunately, the authors of that article stated that, "MOOCs' ultimate place in education is still indeterminate, and any pronouncements are premature" (Pirani, 2013, Past, Present, and Future: the MOOC's Place on the E-Learning Continuum section, para. 10). So, is it still much aMOOC about nothing?

WHAT'S CHANGED SO FAR

The authors conducted another literature review with the same keyword "MOOC" six months later (May, 2014), and it showed only a small growth in the number of real research articles published, although the number of dissertations on the topic of MOOCs increased from 212 to 575 in those six months with subjects such as faculty perceptions of learning spaces, faculty engagement, and migration to e-textbooks. To give this some perspective, we compared publications on the topic of MOOCs and on the use of video-conferencing in online learning. Table 2 below reveals that, while articles on MOOCs are more apparent in the newspapers, trade journals, magazines, the total number of dissertations and scholarly journal articles shows less research attention in comparison. Is this only because videoconferencing has been around longer?

Table 2
Number of Videoconferencing and MOOC Articles by Publication Category to May 2014

Number of publications found in	On Videoconferencing	On MOOCs
Conference papers & proceedings	7	8
Dissertations/Theses	1,357	575
E-Books	21	12
Magazines	10	190
Newspapers	9	576
Reports	--	9
Scholarly Journals (NOT peer-reviewed)	48	99
Scholarly Journals (peer-reviewed)	223	187
Trade Journals	72	522
Newswire feeds	12	263
Total	1,759	2,441

The need for higher quality research and publications appears to be getting some, though not widespread, attention (Reeves & Hedberg, 2014). Several Centers for the study of MOOCs have been established.

For instance, the *MOOC Research Hub*'s home page indicates that, "The proliferation of MOOCs in higher education requires a concerted and urgent research agenda" (MOOC Research, 2014a). Supported by the Bill & Melinda Gates Foundation, the MOOC Research Initiative (MRI) was established "to explore the potential of MOOCs to extend access to postsecondary credentials through more personalized, more affordable pathways" (MOOC Research, 2014b). As part of these efforts from the Gates Foundation, there is a research initiative that offers research grants and a MRI Evidence Hub where researchers can share their work. At this time, however, it is not yet functional and a note at the website suggests that viewers "…stay informed on MOOC news, information, and updates" (MOOC Research, 2014c). Such updates might come from reading the MOOC News and Reviews, OLDaily, Hack Education, The Chronicle of Higher Education, Insider Higher Ed, EdSurge, and e-Literate, none of which are peer-reviewed journals.

So, where are the studies in MOOC learning effectiveness? A June 2014 ProQuest search of only peer-reviewed articles on MOOCs turned up 122 such articles with 116 having been published in "scholarly journals" since January 2013. The search results showed that 18 articles were published in March of 2013 and 16 were published in July 2013. So far, 2014 has seen seven (7) articles in January, two (2) in February, 11 in March, two (2) in April, and seven (7) in May. While such numbers do not denote an abundance of literature, it is a sign that the MOOC research field is beginning to blossom. The journals publishing the majority of these scholarly articles were: *Journal of Online Learning and Teaching* (17 such articles), *Distance Education* (7), *Nature* (5), *College Composition and Communication* (5), and *Academe* (4).

A few special issues of scholarly journals have been published such as the *Journal of Online Learning and Teaching* (Siemens, Irvine, & Code, 2013) with three research papers on MOOCs. The *International Review of Research in Open and Distance Learning* publishes MOOC articles and has plans for a special edition on MOOCs from an international viewpoint. Perhaps these will add to the knowledgebase we are building. At the same time, we should point out that many were not studies examining effectiveness, but were case studies and anecdotal accounts concerning MOOCs (i.e., this is what we did and how we did it).

Once this research evidence of MOOC effectiveness is published, people must be able to find it. ProQuest databases' classification systems do not encompass an accurate categorization upon which to search. Classification of these articles from institutions such as the Massachusetts Institute of Technology, Athabasca University, Duke University, Hampton University, and others show 14 MOOC articles classified under *School and Educational*

Services, 11 as *Experimental/Theoretical*, seven (7) as *Telecommunications Systems & Internet Communications*, and four (4) classified as *Curriculum & Programs & Teaching Methods*. If researchers want to locate articles on MOOC research, they have to ask which of these classifications is most likely to yield useful results.

SO WHAT HAS CHANGED?

As indicated, Liyanagunawardena et al. (2013) found fewer than 70 research articles published in scholarly journals during the period 2008-2012. In addition, our ProQuest literature search revealed only 116 journal articles on MOOCs since January of 2013. While definitely a substantive increase in the research attention on MOOCs, such numbers pale in comparison to the media attention on MOOCs. Many of these research articles are focused on topics such as perceived best practices in MOOCs, personal experiences, development notes, learning analytics, comparisons between delivery systems, and technology support notes on tools such as robo-grading. Although scholarly journals are beginning to publish more MOOC research papers, clearly, there remains an open research gap on the learning effectiveness of MOOCs. In depth analyses of MOOCs are now vital since they can help with administrator and governmental decision-making and funding related to MOOCs and higher education in general.

Some of the questions we asked are being addressed with current studies, but there is a pressing need for researchers to investigate and answer questions like the following:

- What do learning analytics tell us about the factors contributing to learner success in a MOOC?
- To what extent does extending the time-on-task really improve learning in a MOOC?
- How is a MOOC similar or different from general online learning?
- How does social media contribute to learning in a MOOC environment?
- How can peer-review or peer-grading be used to accurately assess a student's ability?
- How can the developers of MOOCs maintain growth and quality in MOOCs?
- What kinds of activities encourage active learning and increased engagement?
- What organizational models, instructional design approaches, and degree of structure best support MOOC students?
- How can instructors in MOOCs most effectively elicit higher order thinking?

With the answers to these and similar questions, MOOCs may indeed reach their potential as effective, innovative learning environments. Although building slowly, the body of research to support this evolution is beginning to grow and may eventually become much aMOOC about something.

References

Anonymous (2013). News from ASIS&T chapter. *Bulletin of the American Society for Information Science and Technology (Online), 39*(5), 12. Retrieved from http://search. proquest.com/docview/1411122064?accountid=13158

Bonk, C. J., & Dennen, V. P. (2005). *Massive multiplayer online gaming: A research framework for military education and training.* (Technical Report # 2005-1). Washington, DC: U.S. Department of Defense (DUSD/R): Advanced Distributed Learning (ADL) Initiative. Retrieved from http://mypage.iu.edu/~cjbonk/GameReport_Bonk_final.pdf;

Breslow, L., Pritchard, D. E., DeBoer, J., Stump, G. S., Ho, A. D., & Seaton, D. T. (2013). Studying learning in the worldwide classroom: Research into edX's first MOOC. *Research & Practice in Assessment, 8,* 13-25

Cavanaugh, J. (2005). Teaching online-A time comparison. *Online Journal of Distance Learning Administration, 8*(1). Retrieved from https://www.westga.edu/~distance/ojdla/spring81/cavanaugh81.htm

Cormier, D., & Siemens, G. (2010). Through the open door: Open courses as research, learning, and engagement" [online], *EDUCAUSE Review, 45*(4), 30-39. Retrieved from http://www.educause.edu/ero/article/through-open-door-open-courses-research-learning-and-engagement

Daniel, J. (2012). Making sense of MOOCs: Musings in a maze of myth, paradox and possibility. *Journal of Interactive Media in Education, 3.* Retrieved from http://www-jime.open.ac.uk/jime/article/viewArticle/2012-18/html/

Davidson-Shivers, G. V. (2009). Frequency and types of instructor interactions in online instruction. *Journal of Interactive Online Learning, 8*(1), 23-40.

Fowlkes, K. (2013, February 5). MOOCs: Valuable innovation or grand diversion?. *InformationWeek.* Retrieved from http://www.informationweek.com/education/online-learning/moocs-valuable-innovation-or-granddiver/240147875

Gaudiosi, J. (2008). Army sets up video-game studio. *Wired.* Retrieved from http://www.wired.com/gaming/gamingreviews/news/2004/06/63911

Harper, E. (2007, July 9). *MMO players make great leaders.* Retrieved from http://wow.joystiq.com/2007/07/09/mmo-players-make-great-leaders/

Hernandez, C. (2014, February 14). *World of Warcraft: An Educational Tool* [Web log post]. Retrieved from https://sites.dartmouth.edu/socy91w14/2014/02/14/world-of-warcraft-an-educational-tool/

Holrer, M. (2013, August 2). MOOCs: Revolutionizing higher ed. *BusinessNorth.com.* Retrieved from http://www.businessnorth.com/viewarticle.asp?articleid=5464

Ifenthaler, D., & Widanapathirana, C. (2014). Development and validation of a learning analytics framework: Two case studies using support vector machines. T*echnology, Knowledge and Learning, 19*(1-2), 221-240. doi:http://dx.doi.org/10.1007/s10758-014-9226-4

Joseph, A. M., & Nath, B. A. (2013, July). *Integration of massive open online education (MOOC) system with in-classroom interaction and assessment and accreditation: An extensive report from a pilot study.* Paper presented at WorldComp 2013, Las Vegas, NV. Retrieved from http://weblidi.info.unlp.edu.ar/WorldComp2013-Mirror/p2013/EEE3547.pdf

Korn, M., & Levitz, J. (2013, January). Online courses look for a business model. *The Wall Street Journal.* Retrieved from http://online.wsj.com/news/articles/SB10001424127887324339204578173421673664106

Liyanagunawardena, T. R., Adams, A. A., & Williams, S. A. (2013). MOOCs: A systematic study of the published literature 2008-2012. *International Review of Research in Open & Distance Learning, 14*(3), 202-227.

Marshall, S. (2013). Evaluating the strategic and leadership challenges of MOOCs. *Journal of Online Learning and Teaching, 9*(2), 216. Retrieved from http://search.proquest.com/docview/1500422691?accountid=13158

Meyer, L. (2013, June 6). California bill allowing credit for MOOCs passes senate. *Campus Technology.* Retrieved from http://campustechnology.com/articles/2013/06/06/california-bill-allowing-credit-for-moocs-passes-senate.aspx

MOOC Research. (2014a). *Welcome to the MOOCResearch Hub.* Retrieved from http://www.moocresearch.com/

MOOC Research. (2014b). *MOOC Research Initiative.* Retrieved from http://www.moocresearch.com/research-initiative/about

MOOC Research. (2014c). *Research Evidence Hub.* Retrieved from www.moocresearch.com/research-evidence-hub/information

Pirani, J. A. (2013, November 4). A compendium of MOOC perspectives, research, and resources. *EDUCAUSE Review Online.* Retrieved from http://www.educause.edu/ero/article/compendium-mooc-perspectives-research-and-resources

Rajabi, H., & Virkus, S. (2013). The potential and readiness of Tallinn University to establish massive open online courses (MOOCs). *Qualitative and Quantitative Methods in Libraries (QQML), 4,* 431-439. Retrieved from http://www.qqml.net/papers/December_2013_Issue/249QQML_Journal_2013_Rajabi_Virkus_4_431_439.pdf

Reeves, T. C., & Hedberg, J. G. (2014). MOOCs: Let's Get REAL. *Educational Technology: The magazine for managers of change in education, 54*(1), 3-8.

Schoenack, L. (2013). A new framework for massive open online courses (MOOCs). *Journal of Adult Education, 42*(2), 98-103. Retrieved from http://search.proquest.com/docview/1490578512?accountid=13158

Siemens, G., Irvine, V., & Code, J. (2013). MOOCs: An academic perspective on an emerging technological and social trend. [Special Issue] *Journal of Online Learning and Teaching, 9*(2) Retrieved from http://search.proquest.com/docview/1500421435?accountid=13158

Saltzman, G. M. (2014). The economics of MOOCs. *National Education Association.* Retrieved from http://www.nearh.org/assets/docs/HE/2014_Almanac_Saltzman.pdf

Savenjie, D. (2013, November). 8 questions MOOCs face in 2013. *Education Dive.* Retrieved from http://www.educationdive.com/news/8-questions-moocs-face-in-2013/75870/

Sumell, A. J. (2013, March). I don't want to be Mooc'd. *The Chronicle Review.* Retrieved from https://chronicle.com/article/I-Dont-Want-to-Be-Moocd/138013/

Williams, V. S. (2014, August 14). Research Today: Results from a PROQUEST search on the term "MOOC" [Web blog post]. Retrieved from http://sites.psu.edu/assessment/2014/08/14/research-today-results-from-a-proquest-search-on-the-term-mooc/

Yuan, L., & Powell, S. (2013). MOOCs and open education: Implications for higher education. Cetis Publications, *Centre for Educational Technology, Interoperability and Standards.* Retrieved from http://publications.cetis.ac.uk/2013/667

Vicki S. Williams serves in the Teaching & Learning with Technology (TLT) department at Penn State where she is Manager, Assessment & Evaluation Research. In this role, she studies and evaluates the effectiveness of technology interventions and their applications to learning and teaching. She received her Ph.D. in Instructional Systems from The Pennsylvania State University and her M.Ed. in Science Education from Edinboro University of Pennsylvania. Before joining TLT, Dr. Williams taught secondary school science and Training and Development at Penn State. Her current research focuses on the use of technologies to facilitate large enrollment courses, in both online and resident instruction.

Nai-Fen Su is a Ph.D. candidate in Workforce Education and Development program and concurrently a M.Ed. candidate in Counselor Education program with a dual emphasis in Rehabilitation and Career Counseling at the Pennsylvania State University. Since 2012, Nai-Fen Su has been working as an assessment graduate assistant in Educational Technology Services (ETS) in Information Technology Services (IST) at Penn State. Until now, she has been involved in over 20 assessment projects in ETS at Penn State. Before studying at Penn State, Nai-Fen Su also worked as an employee relations specialist for 4 years at Qisda Corporation in Taiwan. Her current research focuses on the career development for college students with or with not disabilities, disability employment, recruiters' competencies, and online learning.

International Jl. on E-Learning (2015) **14**(3) Special Issue, 385-399

MOOCs: Redirecting the Quest for Quality Higher Education for All

THOMAS C. REEVES
The University of Georgia, USA
treeves@uga.edu

CURTIS J. BONK
Indiana University, USA
cjbonk@indiana.edu

An argument is presented that the quest for quality teaching and learning in MOOCs should not be limited to merely demonstrating that these innovative learning environments have the same levels of effectiveness as traditional educational approaches (e.g., classroom instruction), but rather that they can actually go beyond current levels of impact. This will require a dramatic change in traditional research goals from those that are focused on providing evidence of "what works" in higher education to educational design research goals that are focused on "how can we make this work and why does it have the effects that it does?"

INTRODUCTION

This special issue of the *International Journal on E-Learning (IJEL)* is focused on massive open online courses (MOOCs), arguably the most controversial development in the application of technology in higher education in the last twenty-five years. As indicated in the Preface and opening article of this issue, in the fall of 2013, more than one hundred scholars gathered in Las Vegas for a preconference symposium on "MOOCs and Open Education Around the World" before the annual E-Learn Conference sponsored by the Association for the Advancement of Computing in Education (AACE). Some of the participants had traveled across oceans to learn more about how MOOCs and open education could improve access, reduce costs, and enhance learning, among other outcomes. In effect, each participant had joined with us in our quest for higher quality education for all.

As mentioned in the introduction, during this one day symposium, an assortment of events transpired to offer insights into MOOCs and open education around the world. For instance, outstanding keynote speakers, Paul Kim and George Siemens, described their cutting-edge research and development initiatives and made recommendations for improving practice. Interactive panel sessions were conducted. Thematic groups were spontaneously formed. And many rich and engaging discussions were had.

Among the highly memorable and spirited aspects of this event was the time spent conversing about MOOC-related stories, insights, and experiences of each of the people who had gathered together in Las Vegas. Fortunately, as you have learned from reading the previous articles in this special issue, some of those conversations were extended into papers that have found their way into this special journal issue. These select pieces provide insights into the teaching practices of MOOC instructors, the instructional design approaches employed, the quality assurance measures guiding design, the forms and types of participant interactions, the associated pedagogical approaches undertaken, the steps involved in the implementation of MOOCs, the emergence of various MOOC-related derivatives whether for supporting remedial writing or some other content area, and, of course, the extant research on MOOCs over the past few years. One issue that virtually all of these topics touched on in one way or another is quality.

THE NEVER-ENDING QUEST FOR QUALITY

Each year, dozens of new technologies are announced, and many of them come with enthusiastic claims for how they will "revolutionize" teaching and learning. Consider the 3D Printer. Here are just a few recent headlines from stories from both commercial and academic sources about their "revolutionary" role in higher education:
- "The Future of Higher Education: Reshaping Universities through 3D Printing" (http://3dprintingsystems.com/the-future-of-higher-education-reshaping-universities-through-3d-printing/).
- "Using 3D Printers to Transform Learning in Undergraduate Mechanical Engineering Courses." (http://curry.virginia.edu/research/centers/castlhe/project/using-3d-printers-to-transform-learning-in-undergraduate-mechanical-enginee).
- "Exciting Developments in Uses of 3D Printing in Education" (http://www.emergingedtech.com/2013/05/exciting-developments-in-uses-of-3d-printing-in-education/).

Implicit (and sometimes explicit) in the seemingly never-ending stream of announcements about the application of new technologies in education is the promise that they will elevate the quality of teaching and learning. The claims and assumptions are also evident in the recent promotion of open educational resources (Tuomi, 2013; Wiley, Green, & Soares, 2012). As illustrated by the articles in this special issue, MOOCs are among the latest such technologies that are much higher on promise than on impact. Williams and Su (this issue), for instance, found that while the research on MOOCs and open education is definitely on the rise, the research results fall far short of the claims and predictions of proponents. The quest for the holy grail of higher quality education for all is replete with impediments. One thing is clear; as our colleagues Insung Jung and Colin Latchem point out, replicating previous outcomes will no longer suffice.

> ...ODL (online and distance learning) providers should no longer simply be concerned with trying to prove their products and services measure up to the standards of conventional education. They should have the confidence – and the evidence – to show that their systems and methods are superior to many of those in conventional education and are particularly well suited to the needs of the knowledge society and Information Age. (Jung & Latchem, 2012, p. 265)

The above quote from Jung and Latchem (2012) was not written specifically in reference to massive open online courses (MOOCs); nevertheless, it is conspicuously relevant to the concerns presented in this special issue. Of the scant research to date on MOOCs, several studies have been aimed at examining whether MOOCs are as good as traditional classroom courses or more conventional forms of online or blended learning (Breslow et al., 2013; Gasevic, Kovanovic, Joksimovic, & Siemens, 2014; Hollands & Tirthali, 2014). Some scholars investigating MOOCs and open education focus on differential attrition rates, whereas others examine grades, test scores, learner satisfaction, or some combination thereof (Bonk, Lee, Reeves, & Reynolds, 2015). There are myriad ways in which researchers today are attempting to answer the inevitable questions posed by educators, government officials, the media, and assorted others as to whether MOOCs and other forms of open education offer similar outcomes to traditional forms of education.

If we heed the advice of Jung and Latchem (2012), however, the entrepreneurs and scholars involved in designing and implementing MOOCs should not aim for mere equivalency; instead, they should seek evidence that these innovative learning environments can actually exceed the outcomes of other approaches to providing higher education. It is not enough for the world of higher education to be open (Bonk, 2009), it must empower people to fulfill their life potential to the greatest degree possible. Each article published on MOOCs and open education, including those in this special issue, should offer some insights into how these new forms of educational delivery are enabling humans to progress in positive directions, not simply replicating what has been accomplished before with previous forms of learning delivery (Veletsianos, 2014).

As indicated from the title and introduction to this article, we are on a quest. Essentially, this quest involves maximizing the extraordinarily high quality learning experience and outcomes that MOOCs have the potential to provide. Admittedly, quality is an extremely difficult term to define (Pirsig, 1975). Global efforts to monitor and enhance the quality of e-learning have been underway for some time (Jung & Latchem, 2012), and it is vital to turn even more attention to the quality of learning outcomes realized through MOOCs. Although some educational researchers and scholars may have argued in the past that the same criteria applied for several decades to traditional modes of higher education delivery can suffice for evaluating the quality of online learning units and programs, the consensus expressed in the current literature emphasizes the desirability of quality assurance approaches uniquely tailored to e-learning (Benson, 2003; Koul, 2006; Meyer, 2002; Moore & Kearsley, 2011; Shelton, 2011; Stella & Gnanam, 2004). The same can be said regarding quality standards for MOOCs (DeBoer, Stump, & Breslow, 2014).

Efforts to define and improve the quality of e-learning in higher education began in the mid-1990s. At that time, various World Wide Web technologies became widely available for interactive online and blended forms of learning. Many of these same technologies have powered the recent explosion of MOOCs and open education. Earlier efforts focused on evaluating the quality of distance education can be traced back at least to the 1930s (Moore & Kearsley, 2011), but quality evaluation schemes have proliferated in recent years due to increasing pressure at institutional, national, regional, and global levels to demonstrate what is now possible. Most often such demonstrations are intended to verify that the quality of e-learning has enriched and enhanced, and perhaps even transformed, higher education (Bonk, 2009).

Three well-known quality assurance schemes for online higher education developed to date are:

- The Quality Matters framework developed by MarylandOnline; a consortium of small and large public higher education providers in the state of Maryland, USA (Shattuck, Zimmerman, & Adair, 2014),

- The UNIQUe certification process developed by the European Foundation for Quality in e-Learning (EFQUEL) (Dondi & Morettim 2007), and

- The QA Scorecard (Shelton & Moore, 2011), a product of the Sloan Consortium (now renamed the Open Learning Consortium).

Table 1 highlights the critical characteristics among the three schemes.

Table 1

Critical Characteristics of Three Schemes for Online Higher Education

	QM Rubric	UNIQUe Guide	QA Scorecard
Source	U.S. higher education non-profit organization initially funded by a U.S. Department of Education grant and now member supported.	European non-profit foundation funded by membership dues.	U.S. non-profit foundation originally funded by the Alfred P. Sloan Foundation and now member supported.
Users	500 higher education institutions in the U.S.	100 higher education institutions, primarily in Europe.	300 higher education institutions, primarily in North America.
Criteria	8 general standards and 41 specific standards.	10 general criteria and 71 specific standards.	9 general categories and 70 specific quality indicators.
Focus	Instructional design of e-learning units.	Institutional "fitness for purpose" and "commitment to innovation."	Online educational programs.
Process	External review by trained peer panel.	External review by professional auditors.	Internal review led by program administrators.
Benefits	Certification and enhancement of individual e-learning units.	Accreditation of the institution.	Foundation for enhanced decision-making by program administrators.
Constraints	Emphasis is on existing instructional design principles rather than cutting-edge, but perhaps risky, innovation.	Re-accreditation must be sought every three years.	The strategic planning focus by administrators may not adequately guide teachers and designers or encourage innovation.

The challenge of providing compelling evidence that the learning opportunities provided by MOOCs exceed many of those found in traditional higher education institutions is formidable. After all, comparisons between online learning and traditional instruction have almost always found either "no significant differences" in learning or statistically significant differences that are not sufficiently educationally significant (Bernard, Abrami, Lou, Borokhovski, Wade, Wozney, Wallet, Fiset, & Huang, 2004; Tallent-Runnels, Thomas, Lan, Cooper, Ahern, Shaw, & Liu, 2006; Tamim, Bernard, Borokhovski, Abrami, & Schmid, 2011). Literally hundreds of research studies have been read, summarized, and compared with little to offer to those seeking such differences.

Given the long history of "no significant differences" found in various forms of research on distance learning, including fully online and blended ones, establishing the superiority of MOOCs in providing 21st Century higher learning opportunities and outcomes will not be easy (Mazoue, 2014). MOOCs add layers of difficulties given their potentially staggering size and fast changing enrollment populations. Many individuals with little desire or commitment to course completion are enrolled in MOOCs, MOOC-like derivatives, and other forms of open online education, massive or not. Those who sign up for MOOCs with the full intention of course completion often find themselves overwhelmed by inadequate communications and vague or nonexistent forms of interaction. As a result, while MOOCs have scarcely been on the academic radar for a few years, some scholars are already labeling them a failure (Baggaley, 2014).

In this paper, we would like to argue that it should be a primary goal of those who engage in the design, development, implementation, and evaluation of MOOCs to find areas wherein they add value to the human experience. We recognize that others may contend that it is sufficient to offer an equivalent higher education learning opportunity that can be accessed more easily at little or no cost. While cost and access are admittedly important issues, these factors are not our focus here. We seek to maximize the quality of the experience of learning in a MOOC and the outcomes thereof.

Of course, any consideration of the quality of MOOCs in higher education today must also acknowledge some of the problems plaguing this sector. The various problems or issues include:

- A perception that the economic and social value of higher education degrees is declining (Arum & Roska, 2011; Delbanco, 2013; DeMillo, 2011),

- Concerns about the growth of unscrupulous for-profit higher education providers (Hentschke, Lechuga, & Tierney, 2010; Mettler, 2014),

- The assumption on the part of some policy makers, especially in developing countries, that open higher education is a second rate education in comparison to traditional universities (Kanwar & Clarke, 2012; Willems, Tynan, & James, 2013),

- The weak motivation of many of today's higher education learners, especially with respect to the conative (volitional) learning domain (Kolbe, 1990; Reeves, 2006), and

- Growing alarm at the increasing costs of higher education (Archibald & Feldman, 2010; Riley, 2011; Rose, 2013)

In the midst of such critiques and concerns, MOOCs and various other forms of open education have arisen, and, not surprisingly, are being advocated as a key solution to these problems by some individuals (Pappano, 2012), while being essentially dismissed by others (Baggaley, 2014;

Kalman, 2014). Unfortunately, most of those suggesting MOOCs as solutions have thus far failed to rely on rigorous research (Gasevic et al., 2014). At the same time, as shown in the article by Williams and Su in this issue, some important strands of research have started to emerge (Hollands & Tirthali, 2014; Kelly, 2014; MOOC Research, 2014), but much remains to be done.

QUALITY ASSURANCE THROUGH EDUCATIONAL DESIGN RESEARCH

It is beyond the scope of this paper to prescribe quality indicators for MOOCs. As described below, this is a project for sustained educational design research (McKenney & Reeves, 2012). Nonetheless, some important preliminary work has been done in this area. For example, Yousef, Chatti, Schroeder, and Wosnitza (2014) used survey methods to identify "74 criteria for effective MOOC environments classified into the dimensions of pedagogy and technology, distributed into 6 categories, namely instructional design, assessment, user interface, video content, social tools and learning analytics" (p. 48). Unfortunately, the utility of the criteria range from quite specific (e.g., "Objectives should be clearly defined at the beginning of each lecture.") to rather vague (e.g., "MOOCs system should provide coaching and scaffolding at critical times."). Whereas the first guideline related to objectives may be easy to do in most MOOCs, the latter guideline related to coaching and scaffolding learning represents one of the major unresolved challenges in all forms of learning, including face-to-face, blended, and online (Fishman & O'Connor-Divelbiss, 2013).

With respect to the question of the instructional quality of MOOCs, Margaryan, Bianco, and Littlejohn (2015) analyzed the evidence of instructional design found in 76 randomly selected MOOCs (50 xMOOCs and 26 cMOOCs). For their analysis, they employed a course survey instrument based on Merrill's (2009) "first principles of instruction." Chief among their findings, Margaryan et al. (2015) reported that they "found that the majority of MOOCs scored poorly on most instructional design principles" (p. 77). This is a useful finding provided that you support the assumption that Merrill's first principles provide a comprehensive foundation for the design of MOOCs. Not everyone agrees, however. For example, Eisenberg and Fischer (2014) suggested that cutting-edge research from the learning sciences could provide a better foundation for the design of MOOCs. Traditional instructional design principles as defined by Merrill (2013) and others may suffice if MOOCs are focused on "learning about," but more complex principles derived from the learning sciences may be required if the focus is on "learning to be" in the sense described by Brown (2005).

Gráinne Conole (2013) from the University of Leicester in the UK criticized the quality of existing MOOCs, including what she described as the behaviorist orientation of xMOOCs and the connectivist orientation of cMOOCs, both of which she concluded have not been successful pedagogically. Conole suggested that the current classification schemes for MOOCs are inadequate. To push the field ahead, she recommended that MOOCs should be categorized along the following 12 dimensions:

1. the degree of openness,

2. the scale of participation,

3. the amount of use of multimedia,

4. the amount of communication,

5. the extent to which collaboration is included,

6. the type of learner pathway,

7. the level of quality assurance,

8. the extent to which reflection is encouraged,

9. the level of assessment,

10. how informal or formal it is,

11. autonomy, and

12. diversity.

Furthermore, she proposed that the 7Cs of Learning Design framework (Conceptualize, Capture, Communicate, Collaborate, Consider, Combine, and Consolidate) "can be used both to design and evaluate MOOCs" (p. 13).

Efforts to improve the quality of MOOCs through survey research methods, content analyses, and critical reviews such as that conducted by Yousef et al. (2014), Margaryan et al. (2015), Conole (2013), and others are laudable. However, additional research approaches and instruments are now required to gain greater insights into aspects of participant engagement, persistence, collaboration, reflection, satisfaction, and overall learning within MOOCs and MOOC-like derivatives. One viable alternative is educational design research (McKenney & Reeves, 2012; Plomp & Nieveen, 2009). It is important to point out that educational design research may also be referred to as design-based research, formative experiments, development research, and by several other terms (van den Akker, 1999).

Educational design research (EDR) is not a methodology per se, but, rather, it is a genre or approach to rigorous inquiry. It starts first and foremost with the identification of a significant challenge or persistent problem related to education. Certainly finding ways of designing and implementing MOOCs that present high quality learning experiences with meaningful outcomes is just such a challenge.

Another distinguishing characteristic of EDR is that it involves close collaboration among educational researchers and practitioners. EDR is not done in a laboratory and then tossed over the real or virtual walls of a physical or online "classroom" with the expectation that it will work. EDR changes the foundational question underlying educational research from "what works?" to "how can we make this work and why?"

EDR has two primary outcomes. First, it ideally yields a robust intervention or treatment. Second, it enables the identification and refinement of new theoretical knowledge, most often in the form of reusable design principles (Kali, 2008). EDR conducted in the context of MOOCs should result in the development of an interactive learning environment that is highly engaging, fosters close collaboration among learners, holds learners to high standards of achievement, and enables participants to develop higher order outcomes related to their goals and objectives. Such research would also allow researchers to identify criteria for ensuring the quality of future MOOCs or other forms of online learning.

EDR proceeds through iterative stages of analysis, prototyping, testing, reflection, and refinement of the treatment or intervention. While it is difficult to fully and accurately represent the iterative nature of EDR in one graphic, Figure 1 presents a generic model for conducting educational design research suggested by McKenney and Reeves (2012). One of the major components of EDR that this illustration as a representation of EDR fails to capture is the truly iterative nature of the evaluation and reflection stage. In effect, these processes of evaluation and reflection are repeated as many times as necessary to produce a maturing intervention. Or alternatively, the research project can be reoriented to another type of intervention if the one being tested does not produce sufficient results.

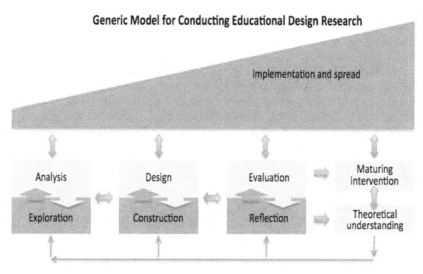

Figure 1. Generic model for the educational design research process (McKenney & Reeves, 2012).

CONCLUSION

In this paper, we have recommended that the quest for quality teaching and learning in MOOCs extend beyond merely demonstrating that these innovative learning environments produce the same levels of effectiveness as traditional educational approaches (e.g., classroom instruction or other forms of online or blended learning). Status quo approaches simply reify existing practices while putting in place low expectations for this potentially transformative form of education delivery. We believe that educators worldwide should be exploring, researching, and implementing educational delivery mechanisms and resources that push the bar for success to higher levels and provide structures or pathways for enhanced quality of education. Bare minimums will no longer suffice. Initiatives related to MOOCs and open education, therefore, should seek to far exceed current levels of impact. To put it another way, just as good is just not good enough for the still emerging phenomena of MOOCs and open education.

While we perceive value in deriving indicators of the quality of MOOCs using existing evaluation schemes (e.g., Shattuck et al., 2014) or through other means of inquiry such as content analysis (e.g., Margaryan et al., 2015), we recommend that the people involved in major MOOC initiatives guide their efforts to improve the quality of the learning experience and outcomes of MOOCs through rigorous educational design research (Van den Akker, Gravemeijer, McKenney, & Nieveen, 2006). Quality is not something just to be found in a MOOC; instead it must be designed into it through painstaking analysis and exploration, highly meticulous and innovative design and construction, and ongoing formative as well as summative evaluation and reflection (McKenney & Reeves, 2012).

As the articles in this special issue indicate, there is much to build upon in this newly discovered land of MOOCs and open education. There certainly is much hope for increasing educational access that can impact learners around the planet at any moment in their life processes. While pragmatic in approach and with many cautions and constraints noted, there is much optimism expressed by the authors of the preceding articles in this issue that we hope you have read or soon plan to read. At the same time, if MOOCs are to maintain and then advance upon their current foothold in different educational territories and provinces, they must clearly demonstrate quality improvements. And if the open education movement, of which MOOCs are now a key part, are to widen the paths to education and make available innovative and exciting educational quests, now is the time to craft our quality gauges. Such measures should not simply be tossed into our educational backpacks as one of many items to take with us in this exciting journey; instead, they should be seamlessly built into part of every discussion that commences, every decision that is made, and every documented research project or detailed publication that appears related to MOOCs and open education around this entire world.

As with each of you reading this special issue, we, Mimi Lee, Curt Bonk, Tom Reynolds, and Tom Reeves, as editors of this special issue, are on a quest to find innovative ways that can provide higher quality forms of education for all. We thank the various scholars who contributed to this issue for joining us on this quest and taking great pains to provide us with an interesting assembly of past experiences as well as keen visions of the future for the field of MOOCs and open education. As their work has revealed, the jury is definitely still out for such new forms of instruction. Nonetheless, we hope that with the E-Learn preconference symposium from 2013 along with this special issue and the comprehensive book that we are currently editing for Routledge on MOOCs and open education around the world (Bonk et al., 2015), that we assisted, albeit in a modest way, toward a better understanding of what MOOCs can offer in this increasingly open educational world. Let the various quests continue!

References

Archibald, R. B., & Feldman, D. H. (2010). *Why does college cost so much?* Oxford, UK: Oxford University Press.

Arum, R., & Roska, J. (2011). *Academically adrift: Limited learning on college campuses.* Chicago: University of Chicago Press.

Baggaley, J. (2014). MOOC postscript. *Distance Education, 35*(1), 126-132.

Benson, A. D. (2003). Dimensions of quality in online degree programs. *The American Journal of Distance Education, 17*(3), 145-149.

Bonk, C. J. (2009). *The world is open: How Web technology is revolutionizing education.* San Francisco: Jossey-Bass.

Bonk, C. J., Lee. M. M., Reeves, T. C., & Reynolds, T. H. (Eds). (2015). *MOOCs and open education around the world.* New York: Routledge.

Breslow, L., Pritchard, D. E., DeBoer, J., Stump, G. S., Ho, A. D., & Seaton, D. T. (2013). Studying learning in the worldwide classroom: Research into edX's first MOOC. *Research & Practice in Assessment, 8*, 13-25.

Brown, J. S. (2005). New learning environments for the 21st Century. Retrieved from http://www.johnseelybrown.com/newlearning.pdf

Conole, G. (2013). MOOCs as disruptive technologies: Strategies for enhancing the learner experience and quality of MOOCs. *Revista de Educación a Distancia, 39*, 1-17.

DeBoer, J., Ho, A. D., Stump, G. S., & Breslow, L. (2014). Changing 'course': Reconceptualizing educational variables for Massive Open Online Courses. *Educational Researcher, 42*(2), 74-84.

Delbanco, A. (2013). *College: What it was, is, and should be.* Princeton, NJ: Princeton University Press.

DeMillo, R. A. (2011). *Abelard to Apple: The fate of American colleges and universities.* Cambridge, MA: The MIT Press.

Dondi, C., & Moretti, M. (2007). *E-Learning quality in European universities: Different approaches for different purposes.* Retrieved from http://efquel.org/wp-content/uploads/2012/03/eLearning-quality-approaches.pdf

Eisenberg, M., & Fischer, G. (2014). *MOOCs: A perspective from the learning sciences.* Proceedings of ICLS 2014. Retrieved from http://l3d.cs.colorado.edu/~gerhard/papers/2014/ICLS-MOOCS.pdf

Fishman, B. J., & O'Connor-Divelbiss, S. F. (Eds.). (2013). *International conference of the learning sciences: Facing the challenges of complex real-world settings.* Florence, KY: Psychology Press.

Gasevic, D., Kovanovic, V., Joksimovic, S., & Siemens, G. (2014). Where is research on massive open online courses headed? A data analysis of the MOOC Research Initiative. *The International Review of Research in Open and Distance Learning, 15*(5). Retrieved from http://www.irrodl.org/index.php/irrodl/article/viewFile/1954/3111

Hentschke, G. C., Lechuga, V. M., & Tierney, W. G. (2010). *For-profit colleges and universities: Their markets, regulation, performance, and place in higher education.* Herndon, VA: Stylus Publishing.

Hollands, F. M., & Tirthali, D. (2014). Why do institutions offer MOOCs? *Online Learning, 18*(3). Retrieved from http://olj.onlinelearningconsortium.org/index.php/jaln/article/download/464/116

Jung, I., & Latchem, C. (2012). *Quality assurance and accreditation in distance education and e-learning: Models, policies and research.* New York: Routledge.

Kali, Y. (2008). The design principles database as means for promoting design-based research. In A. E. Kelly, R. A. Lesh, & J. Y. Baek (Eds.), *Handbook of design research methods in education: Innovations in science, technology, engineering, and mathematics learning and teaching* (pp. 423-438). New York: Routledge.

Kalman, Y. M. (2014). A race to the bottom: MOOCs and higher education business models. *Open Learning: The Journal of Open, Distance and e-Learning, 29*(1), 5-14.

Kanwar, A., & Clarke, K. (2012). Quality assurance in open universities. In I. S. Jung & C. Latchem (Eds.), *Quality assurance and accreditation in distance education and e-learning: Models, policies and research* (pp. 102-112). New York: Routledge.

Kelly, A. P. (2014, May). *Disruptor, distractor, or what?: A policymaker's guide to Massive Open Online Courses (MOOCs)*. Bellweather Education. Retrieved from http://bellwethereducation.org/sites/default/files/BW_MOOC_Final.pdf

Kolbe, K. (1990). *The conative connection: Acting on instinct.* Reading, MA: Addison-Wesley.

Koul, B. N. (2006). Epilogue: Towards a culture of quality in open distance learning: Present possibilities. In B. N. Koul & A. Kanwar (Eds.), *Perspectives on distance education: Towards a culture of quality* (pp. 177-187). Vancouver: The Commonwealth of Learning.

Margaryan, A., Bianco, M., & Littlejohn, A. (2015). Instructional quality of Massive Open Online Courses (MOOCs). *Computers & Education, 80,* 77-83.

Mazoue, J. G. (2014). Beyond the MOOC model: Changing educational paradigms, *EDUCAUSE Review Online.* Retrieved from http://www.educause.edu/ero/article/beyond-mooc-model-changing-educational-paradigms

McKenney, S. E., & Reeves, T. C. (2012). *Conducting educational design research.* New York: Routledge.

Merrill, M. D. (2009). First principles of instruction. In C. M. Reigeluth, & A. Carr (Eds.), *Instructional design theories and models: Building a common knowledge base* (Vol. 3, pp. 3-26). New York: Routledge/Taylor and Francis.

Mettler, S. (2014). *Degrees of inequality: How the politics of higher education sabotaged the American dream.* New York: Basic Books.

Meyer, K. A. (2002). *Quality in distance education: Focus on on-line learning.* San Francisco: Jossey-Bass.

MOOC Research. (2014). *Welcome to the MOOC Research Hub.* Retrieved from http://www.moocresearch.com/

Moore, M. G., & Kearsley, G. (2011). *Distance education: A systems view of online learning* (3rd Ed.). Belmont, CA: Wadsworth.

Pappano, L. (2012, November 2). The year of the MOOC. *The New York Times.* Retrieved from http://www.nytimes.com/2012/11/04/education/edlife/massive-open-online-courses-are-multiplying-at-a-rapid-pace.html?pagewanted=all&_r=0

Pirsig, R. M. (1975). *Zen and the art of motorcycle maintenance: An inquiry into values.* New York: Bantam.

Plomp, T., & Nieveen, N. (Eds.). (2009). *Introduction to educational design research.* Enschede, The Netherlands: SLO. Retrieved from http://international.slo.nl/edr/

Reeves, T. C. (2006). How do you know they are learning?: The importance of alignment in higher education. *International Journal of Learning Technology, 2*(4), 294-309.

Riley, N. S. (2011). *The faculty lounges: And other reasons why you won't get the college education you pay for.* Lanham, MD: Ivan R. Dee.

Rose, S. (2013). The value of a college degree. *Change: The Magazine of Higher Learning, 45*(6), 24-33.

Sharples, M., Adams, A., Ferguson, R., Gaved, M., McAndrew, P., Rienties, B., Weller, M., & Whitelock, D. (2014) *Innovating pedagogy 2014: Open University innovation report 3.* Milton Keynes: The Open University

Shattuck, K., Zimmerman, W. A., & Adair, D. (2014). Continuous improvement of the QM rubric and review processes: Scholarship of integration and application. *Internet Learning Journal, 3*(1). Retrieved from http://www.ipsonet.org/publications/open-access/internet-learning/voume-3-issue-1-spring-2014

Shelton, K. (2011, Spring). A review of paradigms for evaluating the quality of online education programs. *Online Journal of Distance Learning Administration, IV*(I). Retrieved from http://www.westga.edu/~distance/ojdla/spring141/shelton141.html

Shelton, K., & Moore, J. C. (Eds.). (2011). *Quality scorecard for the administration of online programs: A work in progress.* Newbury Port, MA: The Sloan Consortium.

Stella, A., & Gnanam, A. (2004). Quality assurance in distance education: The challenges to be addressed. *Journal of Higher Education, 47*(2), 143–160.

Tamim, R. M., Bernard, R. M., Borokhovski, E., Abrami, P. C., & Schmid, R. F. (2011). What forty years of research says about the impact of technology on learning a second-order meta-analysis and validation study. *Review of Educational Research, 81*(1), 4-28.

Tuomi, I. (2013). Open educational resources and the transformation of education. *European Journal of Education, 48*(1), 58-78.

Van den Akker, J. (1999). Principles and methods of development research. In van den Akker, J., Branch, J. R. M., Gustafson, K., Nieveen, N. M. and Plomp, T. (Eds). *Design approaches and tools in education and training.* Dordrecht: Kluwer Academic Publishers.

Van den Akker, J., Gravemeijer, K., McKenney, S., & Nieveen, N. (Eds.). (2006). *Educational design research.* London: Routledge.

Veletsianos, G. (2014). The significance of educational technology history and research. *eLearn Magazine.* Retrieved from http://elearnmag.acm.org/opinions.cfm?aid=2686761

Wiley, D., Green, C., & Soares L. (2012). D*ramatically bringing down the cost of education with OER: How open education resources unlock the door to free learning.* Center for American Progress. Retrieved from https://www.americanprogress.org/issues/labor/news/2012/02/07/11167/dramatically-bringing-down-the-cost-of-education-with-oer/

Willems, J., Tynan, B., & James, R. (Eds.). (2013). *Global challenges and perspectives in blended and distance learning.* Hershey, PA: IGI Global.

Yousef, A. M. F., Chatti, M. A. Schroeder, U., & Wosnitza, M. (2014). What drives a successful MOOC? An empirical examination of criteria to assure design quality of MOOCs. In *Advanced Learning Technologies (ICALT), 2014 IEEE 14th International Conference on Advanced Technologies for Supporting Open Access to Formal and Informal Learning* (pp. 44-48). IEEE. Retrieved from http://ieeexplore.ieee.org/xpls/abs_all.jsp?arnumber=6901394&tag=1

Thomas C. Reeves, Professor Emeritus of Learning, Design, and Technology at The University of Georgia, has designed and evaluated numerous interactive learning programs. In 2003, he received the AACE Fellowship Award, in 2010 he was made an ASCILITE Fellow, and in 2013 he received the AECT David H. Jonassen Excellence in Research Award. His books include *Interactive Learning Systems Evaluation* (with John Hedberg), a *Guide to Authentic E-Learning* (with Jan Herrington and Ron Oliver), and *Conducting Educational Design Research* (with Susan McKenney). His research interests include evaluation, authentic tasks for learning, educational design research, and educational technology in developing countries. He can be reached at treeves@uga.edu and his homepage can be found at http://www.evaluateitnow.com/.

Curtis J. Bonk is Professor of Instructional Systems Technology at Indiana University and President of CourseShare. Drawing on his background as a corporate controller, CPA, educational psychologist, and instructional technologist, Bonk offers unique insights into the intersection of business, education, psychology, and technology. A well-known authority on emerging technologies for learning, Bonk reflects on his speaking experiences around the world in his popular blog, TravelinEdMan. In 2014, he was named the recipient of the Mildred B. and Charles A. Wedemeyer Award for Outstanding Practitioner in Distance Education. He has also authored several widely used technology books, including *The World Is Open*, *Empowering Online Learning*, *The Handbook of Blended Learning*, *Electronic Collaborators*, and, most recently, *Adding Some TEC-VARIETY* which is free as an eBook (http://tec-variety.com/). His homepage contains much free and open material (http://php.indiana.edu/~cjbonk/) and he can be contacted at cjbonk@indiana.edu.

Association for the Advancement of Computing in Education

Journal Recommendation Form

*Use this form to recommend
that your library subscribe to the*

International Journal on E-Learning

PLEASE ROUTE VIA INTERDEPARTMENTAL MAIL

To: The Serials Librarian at: ─────────────────

From: ─────────────────────

Dept/Faculty of: ──────────────────

Phone: ──────────────────────

I recommend that our library carry a subscription to the following journal published by the Association for the Advancement of Computing in Education (AACE):

International Journal on E-Learning
[ISSN# 1537-2456]

The subscription price for 4 issues is $195 USD
(Add $15 for non-U.S. postage for each subscription ordered).

Date: _____ **Signature:** _____

To place orders, contact AACE or your subscription agency.
AACE, PO Box 719, Waynesville, NC 28786 USA

Abstracts of articles from recent issues are located at:
www.aace.org/pubs